Dress Your Cupcake

Bake Them!   **Dress Them!**   **Eat Them!**

Dress Your Cupcake

Bake Them! Dress Them! Eat Them!

Joanna Farrow

Bounty
BOOKS

First published in Great Britain in 2011 by Spruce
a division of Octopus Publishing Group Ltd

This edition published in 2013 by Bounty Books, a
division of Octopus Publishing Group Ltd
Endeavour House, 189 Shaftesbury Avenue,
London, WC2H 8JY
www.octopusbooks.co.uk

Copyright © Octopus Publishing Group Ltd 2011

An Hachette UK Company
www.hachette.co.uk

ISBN 978-0-753726-64-8
Printed and bound in China

This book includes dishes made with nuts and nut
derivatives. It is advisable for those with known allergic
reactions to nuts and nut derivatives and those who
may be potentially vulnerable to these allergies, such
as pregnant and nursing mothers, invalids, the elderly,
babies, and children, to avoid dishes made with nuts
and nut oils. It is also prudent to check the labels of
prepared ingredients for the possible inclusion of nut
derivatives. Some icings include raw eggs. It is prudent
for the potentially vulnerable (as before) to avoid raw
or lightly cooked eggs. Small candies are suggested as
decoration. Care should be taken if used by or served to
small children.

Publisher: Sarah Ford
Managing Editor: Camilla Davis
Cover design and book development: Eoghan O'Brien
Designer: Michelle Tilly
Photography: Lis Parsons
Food Styling: Joanna Farrow
Production: Caroline Alberti

Glossary

- All-purpose flour = plain flour
- Baking cups = cupcake cases
- Chewy fruit rolls = fruit leathers and winders
- Confectioners' sugar = icing sugar
- Decorating sugar = sanding sugar
- Decorator icing = writing icing
- Dragées = sugar balls
- Fondant sugar = fondant icing sugar
- Glucose syrup = liquid glucose
- Gummy candies = gums, gumdrops, wine gums, etc.
- Hard candies = boiled sweets
- Licorice laces = liquorice whips
- Light corn syrup = golden syrup
- Pastry tip = piping nozzle
- Plastic wrap = cling film
- Semisweet chocolate = plain chocolate
- Shredded coconut = desiccated coconut
- Shredded whole wheat cereal biscuits = shredded wheat cereals
- Superfine sugar = caster sugar

Contents

Making Cupcakes

Take the trend for making and decorating cupcakes to a new level of creativity with this amazing selection of 50 inspiring designs. All the recipes use easy-to-obtain ingredients and decorations. It's the way they're put together that results in the fun. With the exception of Chocolate Cupcakes, which makes enough for six cupcakes, the following recipes all make enough for five cupcakes, but you can easily double or triple the quantities if you want more. Undecorated cupcakes can be stored in an airtight container for up to two days, and are best frozen if stored for any longer. Take care to fill the baking cup with the right amount of cake batter. Too little and there will be a deep space between the risen surface of the cake and the rim of the cups, too much and the mixture will spill out over the cups. As a guide, fill the cups about two-thirds full.

Ingredients

- 5 tablespoons (75 g) lightly salted butter, softened
- 1/3 cup (75 g) superfine sugar
- Generous 1/2 cup (75 g) self-rising flour
- 1 egg, plus 1 egg yolk
- 1 teaspoon vanilla extract

Makes 5

Vanilla cupcakes

1. Line 5 sections of a muffin pan with paper baking cups and preheat the oven to 350°F (180°C).

2. Put all the cake ingredients into a bowl and beat with a hand-held electric beater until pale and creamy.

3. Divide the batter between the baking cups and bake for about 25 minutes until risen and just firm. Leave for 5 minutes, then transfer to a cooling rack to cool.

Ingredients

- 5 tablespoons (75 g) lightly salted butter, softened
- $\frac{1}{3}$ cup (75 g) superfine sugar
- Generous $\frac{1}{2}$ cup (75 g) self-rising flour
- 1 egg, plus 1 egg yolk
- $\frac{1}{4}$ teaspoon baking powder
- Scant $\frac{1}{4}$ cup (25 g) ground almonds
- Finely grated peel of 1 lemon, plus 1 tablespoon juice

Makes 5

Lemon cupcakes

1. Line 5 sections of a muffin pan with paper baking cups and preheat the oven to 350°F (180°C).

2. Put all the cake ingredients into a bowl and beat with a hand-held electric beater until pale and creamy.

3. Divide the batter between the baking cups and bake for about 25 minutes until risen and just firm. Leave for 5 minutes, then transfer to a cooling rack to cool.

Ingredients

- Generous $\frac{1}{3}$ cup (40 g) unsweetened cocoa powder
- $3\frac{1}{2}$ fl oz (100 ml) boiling water
- $3\frac{1}{2}$ tablespoons (50 g) lightly salted butter, softened
- Generous $\frac{1}{2}$ cup (125 g) light brown sugar
- 1 egg
- $\frac{3}{4}$ cup (100 g) plain flour
- 1 teaspoon baking powder

Makes 6

Chocolate cupcakes

1. Line 5 sections of a muffin pan with paper baking cups and preheat the oven to 350°F (180°C).

2. Put the unsweetened cocoa powder in a bowl and whisk in the boiling water. Let cool.

3. In a separate bowl, beat together the butter, sugar, egg, flour, and baking powder with a hand-held electric beater until pale and creamy. Beat in the cocoa mixture until combined.

4. Divide the batter between the baking cups and bake for about 25 minutes until risen and just firm. Leave for 10 minutes, then transfer to a cooling rack to cool.

Making mini cupcakes

Miniature cupcakes are used to build up height in a cupcake design. Double the quantities of your chosen cupcake recipe, and bake 10 in smaller baking cups (see page 24). Bake the large cupcakes first, and reduce the cooking time for the mini cupcakes by about 5 minutes.

Making Buttercream and Other Icings

All the frostings and icings on the following pages are quick and easy to make at home, though you might find it easier to buy ready-to-use rolled fondant, which is available in a wide range of colors.

Ingredients

- 3$\frac{1}{2}$ tablespoons (50 g) unsalted butter, softened
- $\frac{1}{2}$ cup (75 g) confectioners' sugar
- 1 teaspoon vanilla extract
- 1 teaspoon boiling water

Vanilla buttercream

Buttercream is used for covering cupcakes and piping decorations, and also for spreading over the cupcakes before covering with rolled fondant. It's easy to add food coloring to buttercream, and any leftover mixture will keep well in the refrigerator for a few days.

1. Put the butter, sugar, and vanilla extract in a bowl and beat with a hand-held electric beater until smooth. Add the boiling water and beat again until light and fluffy.

Ingredients

- 3$\frac{1}{2}$ oz (100 g) cream cheese, slightly softened
- $\frac{1}{2}$ teaspoon vanilla extract
- Generous $\frac{1}{3}$ cup (50 g) confectioners' sugar

Cream cheese frosting

This frosting is slightly less sweet than buttercream. It's frequently used as a topping for carrot cupcakes, but is also delicious with the other cupcake flavors. Store for up to two days in the refrigerator.

1. Put all the ingredients in a bowl and beat together with a wooden spoon until smooth and creamy. Cover and chill for at least 1 hour to firm up slightly before using.

- Generous ³/₄ cup (100 g) confectioners' sugar
- 2 teaspoons lemon juice or cold water

Glacé icing

This is the simplest icing to make and can be used for spreading over the cupcakes before adding further decorations. If the right consistency is achieved, it looks pretty drizzling down the sides of the cakes, and it can be used for simple, piped decorations, but doesn't hold its shape as well as royal icing.

1. Put the confectioners' sugar in a bowl. (If it has settled in the box and is a little lumpy, it can be sifted first.)

2. Add the lemon juice or cold water a little at a time until the consistency is smooth and the icing just holds its shape. If not using the icing immediately, cover the surface with plastic wrap to prevent a crust forming.

- 1 egg white
- Generous 1¹/₂ cups (225 g) confectioners' sugar

Royal icing

Royal icing sugar is available in some supermarkets, in which case follow package directions for the amount of water to add to make the icing. Royal icing can be stored in the refrigerator for several days, and is ideal for piping decorations. You can also use it instead of store-bought decorator frosting tubes, with the advantage that you can make up any color. Simply beat in food coloring, adding a little at a time until the desired shade is reached, then put in a paper pastry bag (see page 25).

1. Put the egg white in a bowl and whisk lightly to break it up. Add half the confectioners' sugar and beat until smooth.

2. Gradually work in the remaining confectioners' sugar until the icing has a thick, smooth consistency that just holds its shape.

Ingredients

- 3¹/₂ oz (100 g) white chocolate, chopped
- 3 tablespoons milk
- 1¹/₄ cups (175 g) confectioners' sugar

White chocolate frosting

Use this instead of dark chocolate frosting when a pale frosting is more appropriate. If you want something different, but still want the yummy white chocolate flavor, you can always add liquid or paste food coloring.

1. Put the chocolate and milk in a heatproof bowl and rest the bowl over a saucepan of gently simmering water. Leave until the chocolate has melted, stirring frequently.

2. Remove the bowl from the heat and stir in the confectioners' sugar until smooth. Use freshly made.

Ingredients

- 3¹/₂ oz (100 g) semisweet or milk chocolate, chopped
- 2 tablespoons milk
- 3¹/₂ tablespoons (50 g) lightly salted butter
- ¹/₂ cup (75 g) confectioners' sugar

Dark chocolate frosting

This is a delicious frosting for chocolate lovers. Use for spreading over vanilla or chocolate cupcakes as a base before adding further decorations, or you can use it for piped decorations. This frosting is best used freshly made.

1. Put the chocolate, milk, and butter in a small saucepan and heat gently, stirring frequently until the chocolate and butter have melted and are evenly distributed.

2. Remove from the heat and stir in the confectioners' sugar until the frosting is smooth and shiny.

Ingredients

- 1 tablespoon egg white
- 1 tablespoon glucose syrup or light corn syrup
- About 1³/₄ cups (250 g) confectioners' sugar

Rolled fondant

Some of the recipes use rolled fondant as it's so easy to mold and set into various shapes. It can be bought in white and basic primary colors from supermarkets, or in a wider range of colors from specialty cake decorating stores or online bakery and craft suppliers.

1. Put the egg white, glucose syrup or light corn syrup, and about a quarter of the confectioners' sugar in a bowl and mix to a smooth paste.

2. Continue to mix in more confectioners' sugar until it becomes too stiff to stir. Turn the paste out onto the work surface and knead in more confectioners' sugar to make a smooth, stiff paste. (If too soft and sticky the fondant will be difficult to work with.)

3. Wrap tightly in several thicknesses of plastic wrap, unless you're going to be using it immediately.

Using Frostings and Icings

From spreading buttercream to piping royal icing, all the icings used in the recipes are easy to make and use. Here is an overview of the different icing techniques used.

Covering cupcakes with buttercream

Place a spoonful of buttercream on the cupcake and spread it roughly over the surface so it's fairly evenly covered. Using a small spatula, spread the buttercream from the center to the edge so the buttercream forms a smooth covering up to and in between the flutes of the baking cups.

Some recipes, such as the Skull and Bones (see page 124), require a slight dome effect. Once you've covered the cupcake, simply pile a little more buttercream onto the center of the cupcake and spread it down to the edges.

Using rolled fondant

Great fun to use, this icing is soft and pliable. It can be molded or rolled out and cut into any shape. Use a little confectioners' sugar to dust the work surface before you start, or your fingers if molding shapes. This will stop the fondant sticking to the surface or your hands, particularly on a warm day. Any fondant that's not being worked with should be wrapped in plastic wrap, as it quickly dries out and its texture will be spoiled. If the surface dries out because it hasn't been completely sealed, cut off and discard the edges; the center should still be soft and pliable.

Adding color

Some of the cupcake recipes only require small amounts of various colors, so it makes better sense to color your own. Liquid food colors are generally acceptable for adding a pastel shade, but for stronger colors, paste food colors are more effective. Dot the color onto the fondant with a toothpick and knead it in on a surface dusted with confectioners' sugar. Use the color sparingly at first until you're sure of the shade you want. You can always blend in more if you want a more vibrant color. If not using immediately, wrap tightly in plastic wrap.

Blending colors

Basic primary colors can be kneaded together to create more unusual colors. Use the same principle as mixing paints. Red and yellow can be mixed to make orange, blue and red to make purple, red and white to make pink, and black and white to make gray.

Rolling out rolled fondant

When using rolled fondant the trimmings can be rerolled, but wrap in plastic wrap until you need the trimmings so it doesn't dry out.

Lightly dust the work surface with confectioners' sugar and thinly roll out the required amount of fondant. Ideally the fondant should be no more than about $^1/_{16}$ inch (2 mm) thick. Cut out the required shape, then carefully lift the shape over the cupcake and press down gently into position.

Molding rolled fondant

Shapes can also be molded by hand before securing to the cupcakes. A little more skill is required, but it is fun to do and is very like molding modeling clay. Make sure your hands are lightly dusted with confectioners' sugar and the piece of fondant you're molding is smooth and not dried out in places. Use the amount of fondant suggested in the recipe, and mold it until you're happy with the shape. Use the photograph as a guide.

Shaping frills

To create a delicate "frilly" edge such as the Pretty Ballerina's tutu (see page 82), thinly roll and cut out a 3-inch (7-cm) circle of rolled fondant. Cut out a smaller $1^1/_2$-inch (3.5-cm) circle from the center. Cut through the fondant and open it out slightly. Dust a toothpick lightly with confectioners' sugar and run it horizontally along the outer edge of the fondant so the fondant starts to ruffle. Lift the fondant from the surface and redust so the ruffle doesn't stick, then roll the frill with the toothpick again. (The more you roll the toothpick over the fondant, the more ruffled the edge will become.) Trim off the unruffled edge of the strip if it's become uneven. Carefully lift the ruffle from the surface and secure in place. Once positioned, the ruffles can be lifted and folded with the tip of a toothpick.

Dipping shapes in liquid fondant

Shapes molded in marzipan can be dipped in liquid fondant to give a smooth covering. Liquid fondant is made from fondant sugar, which is available in supermarkets. Follow the package directions for the amount of water to add to make the icing. You want a smooth consistency, and it should thickly coat the back of a spoon. Color with liquid or paste food colors, as required.

1.

2.

3.

Push the shape into the fondant and then spoon more fondant over the top until it is completely covered.

Using a large wide-pronged fork or 2 smaller forks, carefully lift the shape, letting the excess drip back into the bowl.

Once most of the excess has dripped off, place the shape on parchment paper and let set for several hours. If a large puddle of icing sets around the base of the shape, cut it off with a small sharp knife. Once set, transfer the shape to the cupcake.

Piping frostings and icings

Buttercream, royal icing, and cream cheese and chocolate frostings are all suitable for piping. It's best to fill the pastry bag shortly before using the icing, otherwise it might dry out in the tip of the pastry bag or the paper may soften and then split. You can use reusable pastry bags fitted with a pastry tip, or you can make your own out of parchment or wax paper.

Making a paper pastry bag

Icings, frostings, and melted chocolate can be piped from a reusable pastry bag or a freezer bag (see page 25). Alternatively, make a paper pastry bag as follows.

1.

2.

3.

Cut out a 10-inch (25-cm) square of parchment or wax paper. Fold it diagonally in half and then cut the paper in half, just to one side of the fold. Take one triangle and hold it with the long edge facing away from you and holding the point nearest you with one hand.

Curl the right-hand point over to meet the center point, shaping a cone.

Bring the left-hand point over the cone so the three points meet. Fold the points over several times so the cone shape is secured in place.

Filling piping bags

Spoon the required icing into the pastry bag, whether reusable, paper, or a freezer bag. (Reusable pastry bags must be fitted with a plain or star pastry tip before use.) Paper pastry bags are easy to use and only require a pastry tip if piping star shapes. For writing purposes, snip off the merest tip so the icing flows out in a thin line. Take care not to snip off too much as the filling will flow out in too thick a line. If using a pastry tip, cut off the end about $^{3}/_{4}$ inch (2 cm) from the point of the bag and insert the pastry tip. Half fill the bag and twist the open end together to secure.

Piping lines and dots

Use a paper pastry bag or freezer bag with the merest tip cut off the point of the bag. Alternatively, use a reusable pastry bag fitted with a fine writer pastry tip. Bought decorator frosting tubes provide a ready-made alternative to filling and using your own bags.

For piped lines, squeeze the bag gently, making sure you keep the open end twisted firmly together so the icing flows out in a steady line. For piping "hair," jiggle the bag slightly as you pipe to make wavy lines. For small dots, hold the bag vertically and apply the smallest amount of pressure so only a tiny amount of icing is piped.

Piping with a star pastry tip

Both paper and reusable bags can be fitted with a star pastry tip for piping. Fit the tip and then fill with icing. For piping stars, hold the bag vertically and squeeze out a small blob of icing, lifting the bag away quickly once the star is the required size. For longer piped shapes, such as Leo the Lion's mane (see page 48), squeeze a larger amount of icing, pulling the bag back from the cupcake gently as you pipe. Gently twist and pull away the bag once the piped shapes are the desired length.

Melting and Using Chocolate

Melted chocolate can be used for piping simple or more intricate shapes and for spooning directly onto the cupcakes. Avoid overheating chocolate or you'll spoil its smooth texture.

To melt on the hob

Chop the chocolate into small pieces and put in a heatproof bowl. Set the bowl over a saucepan of gently simmering water, making sure the base of the bowl doesn't come in contact with the water. Once the chocolate starts to melt, turn off the heat and leave until completely melted, stirring once or twice until no lumps remain.

To melt in a microwave

Chop the chocolate into small pieces and put in a microwave-proof bowl. Melt in 1 minute spurts, checking frequently until the chocolate is partially melted. Remove the bowl and stir frequently until the remaining chocolate has melted in its own heat. Take care when melting white chocolate as the high sugar content makes it more likely to burn in the microwave.

Coloring melted chocolate

For designs such as the Beautiful Butterfly
(see page 42), chocolate can be colored in pastel
shades before use. Only use paste food colors, and
stir in the required amount of coloring once the
chocolate is melted and smooth.

Piping chocolate shapes

Melted chocolate can be piped onto parchment paper either using a supplied template or your own
design. Once piped, it needs to set before the chocolate shape can be lifted from the paper and secured
to the cupcake. If you've filled a bag with melted chocolate and it's started to set before you've used it
all, place the bag in the microwave briefly to soften the chocolate. Don't do this if the bag is fitted with
a metal pastry tip.

1.	2.	3.

Trace the template onto
parchment, then place another
sheet of paper over the top.
Melt the chocolate, put in a
paper pastry bag, and snip off
the merest tip so the chocolate
flows in a fine line. Pipe over
the outline with the chocolate.

Once the outlines are done,
place a craft or popsicle stick
at the bases of the shape so
half the stick is in the middle
of the shape

Fill in the area inside the shape,
easing it into any corners with
the tip of a toothpick. Leave
the chocolate in a cool place, or
refrigerate for at least 1 hour
before peeling away the paper
and securing the chocolate
shape to the cupcake.

Decorating with Candies

Soft chewy candies, gummy candies, and hard candies are all easy to use, and the variety available is great for being creative when decorating cupcakes.

Using candies for decorative detail

Many of the cupcake designs include small candies. Generally, the smaller the candies, the more effective they are for adding finishing touches. Soft fruit chews and gummy candies are easier to cut into small pieces.

Using chewy candies

Chewy candies in pastel colors make great cupcake decorations as they're pliable and can be molded into various shapes. They do, however, slowly soften and loose their shape, so if using don't make your cupcakes more than a day in advance. If you can squeeze the chew between your thumb and forefinger it can probably be shaped without heating. If it's firm, or even brittle, you'll have to heat the candy in the microwave first.

Place the required amount of chews on a piece of parchment paper and heat on full power for a few seconds. The softening time will depend on temperature, amount of sugar in the candy, and how many you're softening at any one time. Some might take a few seconds, others more like 20 seconds, so be cautious.

Once pliable, mold the candy into the desired shape or flatten with a rolling pin, as required. Trim off any edges where necessary and then secure in position.

Using melted hard candies

Hard candies, either clear or colored, can be melted to a thin layer of syrup in the oven to make shapes with cookie cutters as used for Be My Valentine (see page 86) or for snapping into jagged pieces such as used when decorating Mrs Polar Bear (see page 28).

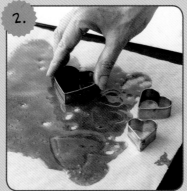

1. Line a baking sheet with parchment paper and arrange the unwrapped hard candies in grid formation, spacing them about 2 inches (5 cm) apart. Preheat the oven to 400°F (200°C), then place the baking sheet in the oven for 5–10 minutes, checking frequently after 3 minutes as some brands might melt quicker than others.

2. While the candy is melting, dip the metal cookie cutters to be used into vegetable oil. Remove the melted candies from the oven and leave for about 30 seconds to firm up slightly. Working quickly, press the cutters firmly into the syrup and lift away immediately so clearly defined shapes are visible. Let cool completely before lifting from the parchment paper and carefully snapping away the excess sweets from the shapes.

3. For shaping jagged pieces of sweet, simply let the melted candy cool completely before snapping into pieces.

General Decorating Techniques

The following pages explain various techniques that are used frequently in the recipes. All are easy to master, even for first-time decorators.

Adding mini cupcakes for height

Slice the dome centers off both large and mini cupcakes. Spread a little buttercream over the large cupcake and invert the mini cupcake on top. Round off the corners of the mini cupcake base with a small sharp knife. Using a small spatula, spread a layer of buttercream over the mini cupcake in a fairly even layer. Clean the spatula and dip in hot water. Let the excess water drip off, then run the spatula gently over the buttercream to smooth it out.

Coloring sugar and shredded coconut

Known as "decorating" or "sanding" sugar, colored sugar makes a useful alternative to candy sprinkles, as you can make any color using paste food colorings. Put superfine or granulated sugar in a small bowl and add a dot of paste food coloring. Using the back of a teaspoon, press the coloring against the side of the bowl so it starts to color the sugar. Continue to work the color into the sugar until evenly blended, adding more coloring paste a little at a time until the desired shade is reached. Use the same technique to color shredded coconut.

Covering cupcakes in decorating sugar

Decorate the edges or entire tops of cupcakes immediately after they are covered with buttercream or frosting. Spread the decorating sugar on a plate and roll those parts of the cupcake you wish to cover in the sugar, turning the cupcake until it is completely coated. Use the same technique to decorate with sprinkles and shredded coconut.

Softening cookies for shaping

Flat, ready-made cookies are good for cutting decorative shapes from. Soften them, one at a time, in the microwave on full power for about 30 seconds, or until the cookie is warm and flexible but not starting to lose its shape. The heating time will depend on the amount of sugar in the cookie and its size, so time cautiously with the first cookie until you've a better indication of how long they take to soften. Use a small sharp knife, craft knife, or cookie cutter for shaping the cookies. You'll need to work quickly as softened cookies turn brittle as they cool. Microwave again briefly to soften, if necessary.

Leaving shapes to harden

Decorations that need to be set before positioning on the cupcakes can be left to set for several hours to harden. Shape them as in the recipe instructions and then leave on the parchment paper for several hours or overnight.

Useful Equipment

Dressing up cupcakes requires minimal equipment. Here are a few useful items that you might have already or want to buy.

Paper baking cups

Although these come in several different sizes, ranging from small "fairy" baking cups to large muffin cases, they are all frequently described as cupcake baking cups on the packaging. The designs in this book are created for cases that measure about $1^1/_4$–$1^1/_2$ inches (3–3.5 cm) in depth and 3 inches (7 cm) across the top in diameter. You can use slightly smaller or larger cases and adjust the designs where necessary. The mini cupcakes are made in cases measuring 1 inch (2.5 cm) in depth and $1^3/_4$ inches (4 cm) in diameter. Both sizes are available in a wide variety of colors, particularly from online baking suppliers.

Cupcake pans

Twelve- or six-cup muffin pans are required for baking cupcakes. Slightly smaller pans are used for baking miniature cupcakes. The cupcakes can't be baked without the pans, as the paper baking cups are not rigid enough to support the cake batter.

Paintbrushes

Fine-tipped paintbrushes are ideal for painting food coloring onto icing. They're also used in some of the recipes for securing decorations in place.

Decorating cutters

Some of the recipes require small round cookie cutters for cutting rolled fondant. These are available in various sizes and give a neat, clean-edged circle, though you can improvise by using a small sharp knife.

Metal spatula

A small, flexible spatula is useful for spreading buttercream, icing, or chocolate frosting over a cupcake when you want a fairly smooth surface before adding more decorations.

Small sharp knife

A small cook's knife is useful for cutting out shapes and for cutting candies into smaller pieces. The sharp, fine-edged tip of a craft knife can be used instead for cutting out small, intricate shapes from rolled fondant where a knife might be less precise. Always work on a chopping board when using as the sharp point can easily damage a work surface.

Rolling pin

A regular pastry rolling pin is fine for rolling out rolled fondant and chewy candies, but for more intricate shapes a smaller rolling pin is easier to manage. Those included in kids' baking kits are ideal, or use a cake decorator's rolling pin, available from specialty stores.

Icing pens

These resemble felt tip pens but are filled with edible food coloring and are useful for painting details onto icing. They can be used while the icing is still soft, but they are easier to use on icing that has hardened.

Freezer bags

A small plastic freezer bag makes a useful, shortcut improvisation for a pastry bag. Spoon the icing into one corner of the freezer bag and twist the bag so the icing is pushed right into the corner with no air spaces. Cut off the merest tip for piping.

Pastry bags

The recipes in this book are designed for using small paper pastry bags. These are disposable, require no tips for piping lines, and are easy to make (see Making a paper pastry bag, page 16). They can also be bought from cookware and cake decorating stores. If you prefer, use washable bags, which are reusable but must be fitted with either a writing or star pastry tip before use.

Pastry tips

These enable you to pipe different shapes onto the cupcakes. They're available in many different designs, although the only ones required for this book are a "star" tip, which can be used to pipe small star shapes or ridged lines, or a "writing" tip for piping straight or curvy lines, eyes, hair, or other more detailed decorations.

Toothpicks

These are useful for dotting paste food coloring from its pot into buttercream, frostings, or rolled fondant, and for supporting shapes while you decorate cupcakes or while the decorations are firming up.

Parchment paper

This is used for making pastry bags (see page 16), for tracing templates, and as a surface for icing and chocolate shapes to harden on, as the paper doesn't stick to the icing and chocolate.

Percy the Penguin

Ingredients

- 5 cupcakes in blue baking cups (see pages 6–7)
- 5 teaspoons orange curd
- 1 quantity royal icing (see page 9)
- 6 oz (175 g) black rolled fondant
- Confectioners' sugar, for dusting
- 10 licorice chews
- Small piece each of orange, white, and red rolled fondant
- 10 pearlized dragées
- Black food coloring
- 5 raspberry gummy drops
- Small handful of white sugar cubes

Equipment

- Small spatula
- Parchment paper
- Scissors
- Rolling pin
- Fine paintbrush
- Small sharp knife

Preparing the cupcakes: Spread the cupcakes with the orange curd using a small spatula. For each cupcake, spoon royal icing on top of the orange curd and spread to the edges. Drag a little icing over the side to form an icicle-shaped point and then continue all around the edge of the cake creating "icicles" of varying lengths. Repeat with the remaining cupcakes.

Penguins: Divide the black fondant into 5 pieces, then mold each piece into an oval shape using hands lightly dusted with confectioners' sugar. Flatten the bases slightly and position on the cakes.

Trace the wing template (see page 127) onto parchment paper and cut out. Soften 10 licorice chews in the microwave for a few seconds if too firm to roll (see page 20), then roll out thinly on the work surface. Place the wing template on a flattened licorice chew and cut around it using scissors. Repeat with the remaining chews. Secure the wings in place with a dampened paintbrush.

For each pair of feet, take a pea-sized piece of orange fondant and cut in half. Flatten each half and make 2 indents using a small sharp knife. Position the feet in front of the bodies. For the chests, thinly roll out the white fondant and cut out oval shapes, measuring about $1^1/_4$ x $^3/_4$ inch (3 x 2 cm). Secure to the fronts of the penguins with a dampened paintbrush.

Faces: Shape small triangular beaks in orange fondant and secure in place with a dampened paintbrush. Push pearlized dragées into the black fondant either side of the beaks for eyes. Paint the centers of the eyes using a paintbrush and black food coloring.

Hats and scarves: Secure a raspberry gummy drop to each penguin's head with a little of the royal icing. Roll tiny balls of orange fondant and place on top of the "hats." Thinly roll out the red fondant and cut out scarves. Wrap around the necks and press gently in place. Cut out 2 shorter lengths of red fondant for the scarf ties. Cut decorative tassels at one end of each length, then secure to the fronts with a dampened paintbrush.

Snow: Lightly crush some white sugar cubes by tapping them gently with a rolling pin. Scatter around the edges of the cupcakes.

Mrs Polar Bear

Ingredients

- 7 oz (200 g) marzipan
- Confectioners' sugar, for dusting
- 3¹/₂ oz (100 g) white chocolate, chopped
- 5 cupcakes in blue baking cups (see pages 6–7)
- 3¹/₂ oz (100 g) clear hard candies
- Blue food coloring
- 1 quantity glacé icing (see page 9)
- 1 oz (25 g) milk chocolate, chopped

Equipment

- Small sharp knife
- 2 Baking sheets
- Parchment paper
- 2 paper pastry bags (see page 25)
- Scissors

Bears: Reserve 1 oz (25 g) of the marzipan and divide the remainder into 5 pieces. Using hands lightly dusted with icing sugar, shape one piece into a smooth oval shape. Press one end firmly down on the surface to flatten, and press the top forward to create a head. Repeat to give 5 heads. Pull off 5 pea-sized pieces from the reserved marzipan, roll into balls, and cut in half. Secure in place on the heads for ears. Roll the remaining marzipan into 10 balls. Flatten each ball on the work surface and square off the sides to shape paws.

Melt the chocolate (see page 18). Coat one of the marzipan head shapes in the chocolate, then lift out on a wide-pronged fork, so the excess drips back into the bowl. Place on a cupcake. Repeat with the remaining heads. Coat the paws in the same way, and transfer to a baking sheet lined with parchment paper. Use the tip of a small sharp knife to make 3 indents along one side of each paw for toes. Leave the heads and paws to harden in a cool place or refrigerate for about 1 hour.

Ice: Line a baking sheet with parchment paper and preheat the oven to 400°F (200°C). Unwrap the clear hard candies and space them 2 inches (5 cm) apart on the paper. Cook for about 5 minutes, watching closely, until they've melted and spread over the paper in a syrupy layer. Let cool completely before breaking into small jagged pieces.

Preparing the cupcakes: Beat blue food coloring into the glacé icing, adding a little at a time until the desired shade is reached. Spoon the icing around the edges of the bears to cover the cupcakes. Arrange the shards of "ice" around the bears, pushing them gently into the icing to hold them in place. Position the paws on top of the ice in front of the bears.

Finishing touches: Put the remaining melted chocolate in a paper pastry bag and snip off the merest tip. Use to pipe claws at the ends of the toes and slightly larger blobs of chocolate for eyes. Melt the milk chocolate, put in another paper pastry bag, and snip off the merest tip. Pipe the centers of the eyes, noses, and mouths.

Mr Hedgehog

Ingredients

- Green food coloring
- 1 quantity vanilla buttercream (see page 8)
- 5 cupcakes in green baking cups (see pages 6–7)
- 6 oz (175 g) pale orange rolled fondant
- Confectioners' sugar, for dusting
- Small piece each of white, yellow, and black rolled fondant
- 4 tablespoons chocolate hazelnut spread
- 5 mini orange candy-coated chocolates
- Red and blue icing pens

Equipment

- Small spatula
- Small sharp knife
- Fine paintbrush
- Paper pastry bag (see page 25)
- Scissors

Preparing the cupcakes: Beat green food coloring into the vanilla buttercream, adding a little at a time until the desired shade is reached. Using a small spatula, spread the buttercream over the cupcakes, peaking it in places to resemble grass.

Hedgehogs: Reserve a cherry-sized piece of the orange fondant and divide the remainder into 5 pieces. Using hands dusted with confectioners' sugar, roll one piece of fondant into a ball, then lengthen the ball into a teardrop shape. Pinch the thin end into a point to shape the hedgehog's snout. Use a small sharp knife to indent small, smiling mouths, then place on a cupcake. Repeat to give 5 hedgehogs.

Secure tiny balls of white fondant with a dampened paintbrush for eyes. Use the reserved orange fondant to shape tiny paws, using a small sharp knife to indent toes. Position the paws beside the bodies.

Put the chocolate hazelnut spread in a paper pastry bag and snip off the merest tip. Pipe a blob of spread on the ends of the snouts and then pipe blobs all over the hedgehogs backs, pulling the pastry bag slowly away as you pipe to create points. Cut the candy-coated chocolates in half and position for ears. Paint the centers of the eyes with a blue icing pen.

Worms: Roll small balls of yellow and black fondant and then press the balls together over the edges of the cupcakes, alternating colors, to shape worms. Paint faces with red and blue icing pens.

Tasty grass

Spiny hedgehog

Cuddly caterpillar

Guess who else is in the garden...

Henry the Hound

Ingredients

- Brown and yellow food colorings
- 1 quantity vanilla buttercream (see page 8)
- 5 cupcakes in black baking cups (see pages 6–7)
- 2 strips of chewing gum
- 5 chocolate-flavored licorice allsorts
- Tube of black decorator frosting
- Small piece of red sugar-coated chewy fruit roll
- 8-inch (20-cm) length of multicolored sugar-coated chewy fruit roll

Equipment

- Small spatula
- Scissors
- Paper pastry bag (see page 25)

Heads and snouts: Beat both brown and yellow food coloring into the vanilla buttercream, adding a little at a time until the desired shade is reached. Reserve 3 tablespoons and spread a thick layer of buttercream over the cupcakes using a small spatula. Place another teaspoon of buttercream in the center of each cupcake and then smooth down lightly to shape snouts.

Faces: Using the photograph opposite as a guide, cut 2 pieces of chewing gum into $^3/_4$-inch (2-cm) widths and secure to the raised buttercream centers leaving a $^1/_8$-inch (2.5-mm) gap between them. Cut the licorice allsorts into thin slices and position for eyes. Pipe centers on the eyes, dots on the cheeks, noses, and mouths in black decorator frosting. Use scissors to cut out small tongues from the red chewy fruit roll. Press gently in place.

Ears: Put the reserved buttercream in a paper pastry bag and snip off the merest tip. Use to pipe long ears down the sides of the cupcakes and plenty of hair at the top of the heads. Pipe an outline of black decorator frosting around the ears.

Collars: Cut the multicolored chewy fruit strip into 5 lengths measuring $1^3/_4$ inches (4 cm). Cut the strips in half if they are very wide. Press the ends into the cupcakes for collars.

Try me too! page 52

WOOF!

WOOF!

WOOF!

WOOF!

What smells
so delicious?

Licking good

Sounds like party time!

Jumping Horse

Ingredients

- 3$^{1}/_{2}$ oz (100 g) white chocolate, chopped
- 1 quantity dark chocolate frosting (see page 10)
- 5 cupcakes in pink baking cups (see pages 6–7)
- 2 round chocolate bars

Equipment

- Parchment paper
- Paper pastry bag (see page 25)
- Scissors
- Toothpick
- Small spatula
- Small sharp knife

Horses: Trace the horse template (see page 126) onto parchment paper. Lay a second larger sheet of parchment paper over the traced outline. Melt the white chocolate (see page 18), then put in a paper pastry bag and snip off the merest tip. Pipe the chocolate around the edge of the horse shape, then slide the top sheet of parchment over a little so you can pipe more shapes. (You'll need 5 in total, but it's worth making a couple extra in case of breakages.) Once all the outlines are done, snip off a little more of the bag and fill in the centers of the horse shapes, spreading the chocolate into the corners with a toothpick. Leave to harden in a cool place or refrigerate for at least 1 hour.

Preparing the cupcakes: Spread the chocolate frosting over the cakes in a generous layer using a small spatula.

Finishing touches: Cut the chocolate bars into 2-inch (5-cm) lengths and position one piece gently into the top of each cupcake, slightly to one side. Carefully peel the parchment paper away from the chocolate horses and rest one on top of each cupcake. Place the front legs over the chocolate bar for support, and push the back legs gently into the frosting.

Other ideas: Use different types of chocolate for the horse shapes and sprinkle green-colored shredded coconut (see page 22) over chocolate frosting for grass. Alternatively, color vanilla buttercream with green food coloring.

Scary Spider

Ingredients

- 1 quantity vanilla buttercream (see page 8)
- 5 cupcakes in orange baking cups (see pages 6–7)
- Tubes of black and red decorator frosting
- 10 large black gummy candies
- 8-inch (20-cm) length of licorice wheel
- 10 small white candies

Equipment

- Small spatula
- Small sharp knife

Webs: Spread the vanilla buttercream over the cupcakes in a smooth, even layer using a small spatula. For each cupcake, pipe a dot of black decorator frosting slightly off center on the buttercream, then pipe lines from the dot to the edges of the cupcake. Each line should be about $1/2$ inch (1 cm) apart. Pipe curved lines between the vertical lines to complete the web. Repeat on the remaining cupcakes.

Spiders: For each spider's body, use 2 large black gummy candies, cutting one in half for the head if the candy is too big. Press gently into the buttercream. For each spider's front legs, cut the licorice into $1^3/4$-inch (4-cm) lengths and then cut these lengths into fine strips, using a small sharp knife. Secure to the back of the "head" with a blob of black decorator frosting and to the cupcake with larger blobs of red decorator frosting. Make and position 6 back legs in the same way, making them $1^1/4$ inches (3 cm) long. Repeat to give 5 spiders.

Faces: Use white candies for the eyes, securing them with black decorator frosting. Pipe large blobs of black decorator frosting in the centers, and pipe smiling mouths in red decorator frosting.

Try me too! page 120

Creepy crawlies

Licorice legs

Scrumptiously scary

You can't scare these three...

Nested Chicks

Ingredients

- 2 large shredded whole wheat cereal biscuits
- 1³/₄ oz (50 g) semisweet or milk chocolate, chopped
- Confectioners' sugar, for dusting
- 3¹/₂ oz (100 g) yellow-colored marzipan
- Several pink and orange fruit chews
- 1 white fruit chew
- Tube of black decorator frosting
- 1 quantity dark chocolate frosting (see page 10)
- 5 cupcakes in pink baking cups (see pages 6–7)

Equipment

- Baking sheet
- Parchment paper
- Teaspoon
- Rolling pin
- Small sharp knife
- Small spatula

Nests: Break the shredded whole wheat cereal biscuits into small pieces and scatter over a baking sheet lined with parchment paper. Melt the chocolate (see page 18). Using a teaspoon, drizzle lines of melted chocolate back and forth over the cereal so some of the chocolate coats the cereal and some drizzles over the parchment paper. Leave to harden in a cool place or refrigerate for about 1 hour.

Chicks: Using hands lightly dusted with confectioners' sugar, roll the marzipan into cherry-sized balls. (You'll need 15 in total.) Soften the pink and orange fruit chews briefly in the microwave if too firm to roll (see page 20). Roll out the pink chews until they are about ¹/₈ inch (2.5 mm) thick, then cut out ¹/₂-inch (1-cm) squares. (You'll need 15 in all.) Make deep cuts along one side of each square with a small sharp knife and fan out, then press one piece onto each marzipan ball. For the beaks, roll out the orange chews to a similar thickness, and cut out 15 diamond shapes. Bend the diamonds to shape beaks and position on the chicks. Soften the white fruit chew in the microwave for a few seconds if too firm to mold, then roll out tiny balls for eyes and secure. Pipe the centers of the eyes in black decorator frosting.

Finishing touches: Spread the chocolate frosting over the cupcakes using a small spatula. Peel the parchment away from the chocolate and cereal mix, and break it into small pieces. Arrange around the edges of the cupcakes to look like nests. Gently press 3 chicks into the center of each cupcake.

Other ideas: Make more nests in the same way and fill with candy-coated chocolate eggs, rather than the chicks.

CHEEP!

CHEEEEP!

CHEEP!

Pointy beak

Crunchy nest

Oliver the Octopus

Ingredients

- 1 quantity vanilla buttercream (see page 8)
- 5 cupcakes in green baking cups (see pages 6–7)
- $2^3/_4$ oz (75 g) green decorating sugar (see page 22)
- 1 lb (450 g) blue rolled fondant
- Confectioners' sugar, for dusting
- 5 birthday candles (optional)
- Small piece of white rolled fondant
- 10 small chocolate drops
- Tube of red decorator frosting
- Black food coloring
- 5 pieces of licorice
- Small piece of orange rolled fondant

Equipment

- Small spatula
- Small sharp knife
- Fine paintbrush

Preparing the cupcakes: Using a small spatula, spread vanilla buttercream over the cupcakes as smoothly as possible. Put the decorating sugar on a plate and gently roll the cupcakes in the sugar until completely coated.

Octopuses: For each octopus, take $1^1/_2$ oz (40 g) of blue fondant and roll into an oval shape using hands lightly dusted with confectioners' sugar. Cut a thin slice off the base and position the "head" on the cupcake. Take $1^3/_4$ oz (50 g) of blue fondant and cut into 8 pieces. On a surface dusted with confectioners' sugar, roll each piece under your fingers into a tentacle shape, tapering to a point at one end and cutting a slice off the other end. Secure the thick ends to the base of the head using a dampened paintbrush. Curve the tapered ends out in different directions. Wrap one of the tentacles around a birthday candle, pushing the end of the candle down slightly into the cake, if liked. Repeat to give 5 octopuses.

Faces: For each face, shape 2 small pieces of white fondant into eyes and secure in place with a dampened paintbrush. Secure a chocolate drop to each eye with a dot of red decorator frosting. Use a paintbrush and black food coloring to paint the outline of a smiling mouth. Fill in the center with red decorator frosting.

Finishing touches: Cut pieces of licorice into "top hats" and secure in place with decorator frosting. Shape and secure orange fondant "bow ties."

Other ideas: Cover additional cupcakes with buttercream in varying shades of blue, and decorate with an assortment of gummy "fish" candies and curls of green chewy fruit roll for seaweed.

Beautiful Butterfly

Ingredients

- 3½ oz (100 g) white chocolate, chopped
- Yellow and green paste food colorings
- 10 orange candy-coated chocolates
- 10 mini orange candy-coated chocolates
- 1 quantity white chocolate frosting (see page 10)
- 5 cupcakes in yellow baking cups (seep pages 6–7)
- Plenty of yellow candy-coated chocolates
- 5 large black jelly beans
- 5 small purple or black gummy candy drops

Equipment

- Parchment paper
- 2 paper pastry bags (see page 25)
- Scissors
- Toothpick
- Small spatula

Butterflies: Trace a right and a left butterfly wing template (see page 127) onto parchment paper. Lay a second larger sheet of parchment paper over the traced outlines. Melt the white chocolate (see page 18), and divide between 2 bowls. Add yellow food color to one bowl of melted chocolate, adding a little at time until the desired shade is reached. Color the other bowl of melted chocolate with green food coloring. Put the chocolate in paper pastry bags, and snip the merest tip off the pastry bag with the green chocolate. Pipe chocolate around the edges of the wings. Slide the top sheet of parchment over a little so you can pipe more wings. (You'll need 5 sets in total, but it's worth making a couple extra in case of breakages.)

Once all the outlines are done, fill in the centers with more chocolate, spreading it into the corners with a toothpick. Snip the merest tip of the paper pastry bag with the yellow chocolate, and pipe a line that joins the ends of the green chocolate. Fill in the centers with more piping using the same technique. While the chocolate is still soft, push one large and one mini orange candy-coated chocolate into the yellow areas of each butterfly wing. Leave to harden in a cool place or refrigerate for at least 1 hour.

Preparing the cupcakes: Spread the chocolate frosting over the cupcakes using a small spatula and arrange a circle of yellow candy-coated chocolate around the edges.

Finishing touches: Peel the parchment away from the butterfly wings and secure in pairs on the cupcakes, leaving a ¼-inch (5-mm) gap between them. (Use extra beans to hold the wings in position, if necessary.) Position one large jelly bean and one gummy candy drop between each pair of wings for bodies.

Jelly bean belly!

Candy wings

Ready to fly away?

Guess who else is coming to play...

Hopping Kangaroo

Ingredients

- 6 ice cream cones
- Confectioners' sugar, for dusting
- $3^{1}/_{2}$ oz (100 g) chocolate-flavored rolled fondant
- $5^{1}/_{4}$ oz (150 g) milk chocolate, chopped
- 5 cupcakes in brown baking cups (see pages 6–7)
- 5 brown candy-coated peanuts
- Several mini marshmallows
- Tubes of black and red decorator frosting
- Handful of yellow and green sugar-coated gummy candies

Equipment

- Serrated knife
- Rolling pin
- Small sharp knife
- Small spatula

Kangaroos: Measure 3 inches (7 cm) from the point of the ice cream cones and slice off the excess with a serrated knife. Slice off the point about $^{1}/_{2}$ inch (1 cm) from the tip and stand the cones upright. Using fingers lightly dusted with confectioners' sugar, take a cherry-sized ball of chocolate-flavored rolled fondant, lengthen it into an oval shape and press onto the top of a cone, pushing the front of the fondant down slightly. Take 2 small pieces of fondant, shape into pointed ears, and position. Roll out the fondant until about $^{1}/_{16}$ inch (2 mm) thick, then cut out a rectangle measuring about $1^{1}/_{4}$ x $^{3}/_{4}$ inches (3 x 2 cm). Secure to the front of the cone for an open pouch. Shape short arms and secure to the sides of the cone. Repeat to give 5 heads, pouches, and pairs of arms.

Melt the chocolate (see page 18). Let cool slightly, then spread a little melted chocolate over the cupcakes using a small spatula. Hold a kangaroo shape over the chocolate and spoon over the chocolate until coated, letting the excess chocolate drip back into the bowl. Position on a cupcake and then cover the remainder in the same way. Spread any remaining chocolate around the edges of the cupcakes.

Joeys: Push a candy-coated peanut into each pouch. Cut small pieces of marshmallow and position for eyes. Pipe the centers of the eyes and snouts in black decorator frosting and mouths in red decorator frosting. Finish the kangaroos' faces in the same way.

Grass: Cut the sugar-coated gummy candies into thin slices and arrange around the edges of the cupcakes.

Try me too! page 70

Chocolate mom

Little peanut joey

Gummy grass

Mack the Monkey

Ingredients

- Blue food coloring
- 1 quantity cream cheese frosting (see page 8)
- 5 cupcakes in black baking cups (see pages 6–7)
- 2³/₄ oz (75 g) milk chocolate, chopped
- 2³/₄ oz (75 g) white chocolate, chopped
- 10 blue candy-coated chocolates
- 2 red candied cherries
- 10 brown candy-coated chocolates

Equipment

- Small spatula
- Parchment paper
- Scissors
- 2 paper pastry bags (see page 25)
- Small sharp knife

Preparing the cupcakes: Beat blue food coloring into the cream cheese frosting, adding a little at a time until the desired shade is reached. Using a small spatula, spread over the cupcakes as smoothly as possible.

Faces: Trace the monkey template (see page 126) onto parchment paper and cut out. Melt the milk chocolate (see page 18). Place in a paper pastry bag and snip off the merest tip. Lay the template on one of the cupcakes and pipe around the edges with the melted chocolate. Carefully lift the template and pipe the outlines on the remaining 4 cupcakes in the same way. Using the template as a guide, pipe an inner line of chocolate to frame the eyes and cheeks, then fill the space between the lines with more chocolate.

Melt the white chocolate, put in a paper pastry bag, snip of the merest tip, and use to fill in the centers of the faces. Pipe smiling mouths and noses with milk chocolate. While the chocolate is still soft, press blue candy-coated chocolates onto each cupcake for eyes and pipe the centers of the eyes in milk chocolate. Cut small semicircles out of candied cherries and secure for mouths. Press brown candy-coated chocolates into the buttercream for ears.

Other ideas: Cover more cupcakes with blue- or green-colored frosting, and decorate with bunches of bananas and leaves cut out of yellow and green rolled fondant.

Leo the Lion

Ingredients

- 5 cupcakes in orange or yellow baking cups (see pages 6–7)
- 1 quantity vanilla buttercream (see page 8)
- 4 tablespoons smooth peanut butter
- Brown food coloring
- 3 or 4 orange fruit chews
- Tube of black decorator frosting
- 5 white mini marshmallows
- 10 blue or purple mini candy-coated chocolates

Equipment

- Small sharp knife
- Large pastry bag
- Small star pastry tip

Preparing the cupcakes: Cut the dome off the top of each cupcake and reserve. Spoon a blob of vanilla buttercream onto the center of each cupcake.

Manes: Divide the remaining buttercream between 2 bowls. Beat the peanut butter into one bowl of buttercream and brown food coloring into the other, adding a little at a time until the desired shade is reached. Fit a large pastry bag with a star tip. Spoon the peanut butter-flavored buttercream into one side of the bag and the colored buttercream into the other. Pipe the buttercream around the edges of the cupcakes as shown in the picture, letting each line trail off to a point to shape a mane. Gently press the reserved cake domes onto the centers of the cupcakes.

Ears: Soften the fruit chews in the microwave for a few seconds if too firm to mold (see page 20). For each set of ears, take 2 pea-sized pieces of fruit chew and flatten into oval shapes. Slice off the bases and position for ears. Pipe an oval shape in the center of each ear with black decorator frosting.

Faces: For each pair of eyes, cut 2 slices of marshmallow and secure in place with dots of decorator frosting. Secure candy-coated chocolates in the centers with dots of decorator frosting. Use black decorator frosting to pipe eyebrows, noses, mouths, and freckles.

Try me too! page 94

RRRRRRRRRRRAAAAAARRRRRR!!

Buttercream mane

King of the kitchen

Harry the Hippo

Ingredients

- 1³/₄ oz (50 g) dark green rolled fondant
- Confectioners' sugar, for dusting
- 1³/₄ oz (50 g) blue rolled fondant
- 1³/₄ oz (50 g) white rolled fondant
- 5 cupcakes in green baking cups (see pages 6–7)
- ¹/₂ quantity vanilla buttercream (see page 8)
- 1³/₄ oz (50 g) gray rolled fondant
- Small piece of pink rolled fondant
- Approximately 10 mini marshmallows
- 10 small blue candy-coated chocolates
- Green chewy fruit roll

Equipment

- Baking sheet
- Parchment paper
- Rolling pin
- 3-inch (7-cm) round cookie cutter
- Small spatula
- Fine paintbrush

Grass: Roll out thin sausage-shaped lengths of green fondant on a surface lightly dusted with confectioners' sugar. Cut into shorter lengths between 1¹/₄ and 2¹/₂ inches (3 and 6 cm)—you'll need about 30 altogether. Transfer to a baking sheet lined with paper parchment, then leave to harden for at least 3 hours.

Water: To create a marbled effect for the water, dust the palms of your hands with confectioners' sugar and roll the blue fondant until about 8 inches (20 cm) long. Do the same with the white fondant and then roll the two lengths together. Fold the fondant over lengthwise and roll. Fold and roll once more, then roll out with a rolling pin until about ¹/₁₆ inch (2 mm) thick. Cut out 5 disks using a 3-inch (7-cm) round cookie cutter. Using a small spatula, spread the cupcakes with a thin layer of vanilla buttercream, then position one fondant disk on top of each cupcake.

Faces: Divide the gray fondant into 5 pieces. From each piece, reserve a tiny ball of fondant for the ears. For each hippo, shape two-thirds of the fondant into a ball and flatten slightly into a rectangular shape with curved edges. Press down gently onto the blue fondant to the front of the cupcake, securing with a dampened paintbrush. Shape the remaining third into the snout, pushing 2 deep holes into the fondant with the end of a paintbrush to create the nostrils. Secure in place, as in the picture, using a dampened paintbrush.

Shape and position the ears, adding a tiny, flattened ball of pink fondant to each. Cut slices of marshmallow for the eyes and secure in place with dots of buttercream. Secure blue candy-coated chocolates for eyes and small pieces of white marshmallow for teeth with buttercream. Repeat to give 5 hippos.

Finishing touches: Press holes into the blue fondant behind each hippo using the end of the paintbrush. Gently press lengths of "grass" into the holes. Cut the chewy fruit roll into ³/₄-inch (2-cm) wide strips and loop the lengths around the grass.

Burrowing Mole

Ingredients

- 5 mini cupcakes (see page 7)
- 3½ oz (100 g) milk chocolate, chopped
- 5 cupcakes in pink baking cups (see pages 6–7)
- 6 tablespoons green-colored shredded coconut (see page 22)
- 1 oz (25 g) semisweet chocolate
- 2 pink fruit chews
- Small piece of black rolled fondant (or 1 large piece of plain licorice)
- Tube of black decorator frosting

Equipment

- Small sharp knife
- Spatula
- Grater

Mole heads: Remove the baking cups from the mini cupcakes, invert them, and then trim off the edges and cut a sloping edge for the backs of the heads. Melt the milk chocolate (see page 18). Place one of the head shapes on a wide-pronged fork over the bowl of melted chocolate, then spoon over the chocolate until it is completely coated. Let the excess chocolate drip back into the bowl. Transfer each coated "head" to the top of a large cupcake.

Grass: Spread the remaining chocolate around the edges of the larger cupcakes using a small spatula, and scatter with the green-colored shredded coconut to resemble grass.

Mole hills: Finely grate the semisweet chocolate and spoon around the mole heads.

Hands and faces: Soften the fruit chews in a microwave for a few seconds if too firm to mold (see page 20). For each mole, take 2 pea-sized balls of the fruit chew and flatten slightly. Using a small sharp knife, make 3 deep indents in each piece to shape paws. Press into position, securing with dots of leftover melted chocolate. Shape small pointed noses from black rolled fondant or a piece of licorice and press into place, securing with dots of decorator frosting if the chocolate has already set. Pipe eyes in black decorator frosting. Repeat to give 5 moles.

Try me too! page 68

Just popping by

Playtime fun

Keep off the grass!

Mischievous Mouse

Ingredients

- Yellow food coloring
- 1 quantity royal icing (see page 9)
- 5 cupcakes in yellow baking cups (see pages 6–7)
- 1 tablespoon lemon curd
- Confectioners' sugar, for dusting
- 9 oz (250 g) brown or chocolate-flavored rolled fondant
- 10 brown candy-coated chocolates
- 1 white fruit chew
- Black food coloring

Equipment

- Small sharp knife
- Teaspoon
- Small spatula
- Small round-handled kitchen utensils of various sizes
- Fine paintbrush

Cheese: Beat the yellow food coloring into the royal icing, adding a little at a time until the desired shade is reached. Cut the dome top off each cupcake to create a flat surface. Spread the lemon curd over the sponge with the back of a teaspoon. Using a small spatula, spread the royal icing over the top of the cupcakes in a smooth layer. Leave for about 30 minutes to firm up slightly. Coat the round-handle ends of a variety of small kitchen utensils in confectioners' sugar and press them gently into the "cheese" to make holes. Turn and lift the utensils to remove.

Mice: Reserve $1^3/4$ oz (50 g) of the brown or chocolate-flavored rolled fondant. Divide the remaining fondant into 5 pieces and then, using hands lightly dusted with confectioners' sugar, mold each into a teardrop shape with a small point at one end. Press 2 candy-coated chocolates into the fondant near the pointed end for ears. Position the "mice" on the cupcakes. Shape 5 long tails from the reserved fondant, tapering each length to a point at one end. Secure to the mice with a dampened paintbrush, letting the tails curl around the edges of the cupcakes.

Faces: Soften the white fruit chews in the microwave for a few seconds if too firm to mold (see page 20). Pull off pieces and roll into 10 miniature balls. Secure in place on the mice for eyes. Paint the centers of the eyes, noses, and mouths using a paintbrush and black food coloring.

Wormy Apple

Ingredients

- 5 cupcakes in red baking cups (see pages 6–7)
- 5 mini cupcakes (see page 7)
- Double quantity vanilla buttercream (see page 8)
- Red food coloring
- 5 green gummy candies
- 5 gummy candy "worms"
- Tubes of black and red decorator frosting

Equipment

- Small sharp knife
- Small spatula
- Round-handled teaspoon

Preparing the cupcakes: Cut the dome tops off each of the cupcakes. Using a small spatula, spread a little vanilla buttercream over the larger cupcakes. Invert a mini cupcake onto the top of each, remove the baking cup, and round off the edges to create a dome shape. Cut out small holes near the tops to create apple shapes. Use a teaspoon to scoop out a small area on the side of each cupcake to represent the "worm-eaten" area.

Apples: For the apple flesh, spread a little buttercream over the scooped out areas of the cakes. Beat red food coloring into the remaining buttercream, adding a little at a time until the desired shade is reached. Using a small spatula, spread red buttercream in an even layer over each of the cupcakes leaving the worm-eaten area free. Once they are all covered, clean the spatula and dip it in hot water. Smooth out the buttercream with the warmed knife. Warm the handle end of a teaspoon in the same way and press around the edges of the worm-eaten holes to resemble teeth marks.

Finishing touches: Cut the green gummy candies into 5 stalk shapes and push into the tops of the apples. Position a gummy candy "worm" on each cupcake, painting on eyes and mouths in black and red decorator frosting.

Candy leaves

That apple was
so delicious

Take a bite out of
me anytime

where is Wormy going next?

Flower Garden

Ingredients

- Green food coloring
- 1 quantity vanilla buttercream (see page 8)
- 5 cupcakes in green baking cups (see pages 6–7)
- Handful of pink mini marshmallows
- Plenty of pink, lilac, and yellow mini candy-coated chocolates
- Tube of white decorator frosting
- Pearlized multicolored sprinkles

Equipment

- Small spatula
- Scissors

Preparing the cupcakes: Beat green food coloring into the vanilla buttercream, adding a little at a time until the desired shade is reached. Spread over the cupcakes using a small spatula.

Marshmallow flowers: Use scissors to cut the marshmallows into thin slices. Make flower shapes on top of each cupcake by arranging 5 or 6 pieces of marshmallow in circles, pressing them gently into the buttercream. Press a small candy-coated chocolate into the centers. You will want 2 or 3 completed marshmallow flowers on each cupcake.

Candy flowers: To make each candy flower, arrange 5 mini candy-coated chocolates of the same color in a circle, pressing them gently into the buttercream. Pipe large dots of white decorator frosting into the space in the center and then scatter the frosting with the multicolored sprinkles while the frosting is still soft.

Try me too! page 26

Beautiful flowers

Marshmallow petals

Christmas Rose

Ingredients

- 5$\frac{1}{4}$ oz (150 g) white rolled fondant
- Confectioners' sugar, for dusting
- 1 quantity dark chocolate frosting (see page 10)
- 5 cupcakes in purple or red baking cups (see pages 6–7)
- Tube of yellow decorator frosting
- 2–3 pale pink flat chews

Equipment

- Aluminum foil
- Baking sheet
- Rolling pin
- 1$\frac{1}{2}$-inch (3.5-cm) round cookie cutter
- Small spatula
- Small sharp knife

Rose petals: Crumple a large sheet of aluminum foil and place on a small baking sheet. (The pockets and folds of the foil will enable the petals to set in curved shapes.) For each rose, roll out one-fifth of the white rolled fondant on a surface lightly dusted with confectioners' sugar, then cut out 5 disks using a 1$\frac{1}{2}$-inch (3.5-cm) cookie cutter. Lightly dust your fingers with confectioners' sugar and lift up one of the disks. Press your thumb into the center, mold the edges around your thumb to create a concave shape, then bend the edges of the petal to look more realistic. Place on the crumpled aluminum foil so the folds of the foil support the fondant petal. Repeat with the remaining 4 disks. Make 4 more sets of petals in the same way, plus a few spares out of any leftover fondant, in case of breakages. Leave for several hours to harden.

Preparing the cupcakes: Using a small spatula, spread the chocolate frosting generously over the cupcakes.

Finishing touches: Arrange 5 petals in an overlapping circle on each cupcake, leaving a small gap in the center. Press the petals carefully down into the frosting, then pipe plenty of yellow decorator frosting into the center of each rose. For the stamens, cut out 5 rectangles from the pale pink flat chews, each measuring about $\frac{1}{2}$ x $\frac{3}{4}$ inches (1 x 2 cm). Make deep cuts along one of the long edges, then roll up from one of the short ends. Press gently into the yellow decorator frosting on each cake.

Sweet centered

Gorgeous petals

Delicate flower

Over the Rainbow

Ingredients

- 5 each of deep pink, pale pink, yellow and cream fruit chews
- Blue food coloring
- 1 quantity vanilla buttercream (see page 8)
- 5 cupcakes in blue baking cups (see pages 6–7)
- 2 teaspoons confectioners' sugar
- $5^1/_4$ oz (150 g) cream cheese

Equipment

- Parchment paper
- Small spatula
- 2 paper pastry bags (see page 25)
- Scissors

Rainbows: For each rainbow, unwrap a chew in each color and soften in the microwave for a few seconds if too firm to mold (see page 20). Roll each chew between the palms of your hands into a long thin strip and then press the colors gently together, bending them into a curved shape. Flatten slightly and slice off the ends. Leave to harden on a sheet of parchment paper.

Preparing the cupcakes: Beat blue food coloring into the vanilla buttercream, a little at a time until the desired shade is reached. Using a small spatula, spread buttercream over each cupcake as smoothly as possible, doming it slightly in the center.

Clouds: Beat the confectioners' sugar into the cream cheese. Place 1 tablespoon in one of the paper pastry bags and the remainder in the other. Cut about $^1/_4$ inch (5 mm) off the end of the fuller bag and pipe fluffy clouds on one side of each cupcake.

Raindrops: Snip the merest tip off the other paper pastry bag and use to pipe tiny raindrops over the buttercream and down the sides of the cupcakes. Gently press the rainbows in position.

Try me too! page 114

Colorful rainbow

Fluffy clouds

Rainy-day baking

Ice Cream Soda

Ingredients

- $5^1/4$ oz (150 g) white rolled fondant
- Confectioners' sugar, for dusting
- $1^3/4$ oz (50 g) red rolled fondant
- $1^3/4$ oz (50 g) red decorating sugar (see page 22)
- 1 teaspoon clear honey
- 5 cupcakes in white baking cups (see pages 6–7)
- 10 clear hard candies
- 1 quantity vanilla buttercream (see page 8)
- 5 fresh strawberries

Equipment

- Teaspoon
- Baking sheet
- Parchment paper
- Rolling pin
- Small sharp knife
- Freezer bag
- Hammer (optional)
- Pastry bag
- Small star pastry tip
- Fine paintbrush

Ice cream scoops: Using a teaspoon, shave off a small piece of the white rolled fondant from the block as though using an ice cream scoop. The slightly textured surface of the fondant will resemble that of ice cream. Tuck the edges under and transfer to a baking sheet lined with parchment paper. Shape 9 more "scoops" in the same way.

Straws: Roll out the white fondant trimmings on a surface lightly dusted with confectioners' sugar until about $1/4$ inch (5 mm) thick. Roll out the red fondant to a similar size. Twist the two lengths together and then reroll under your hands to create a candy stripe effect. Cut into varying lengths between 2 and 3 inches (5 and 7 cm) and transfer to the sheet. You will need a total of 10 "straws." Leave to harden for at least 2 hours or overnight.

Sugar rims: Scatter the red decorating sugar on a small plate. In a small bowl, mix the honey with 1 teaspoon of water, then dip your finger into the honey syrup and lightly coat the top edges of the cupcake baking cups. Roll the edges in the decorating sugar until coated.

Ice cubes: Put the clear hard candies in a freezer bag and beat with the tip of a rolling pin or hammer until lightly crushed.

Finishing touches: Put the buttercream in a pastry bag fitted with a star pastry tip. Pipe swirls of buttercream over each of the cupcakes, piling it up slightly in the center. Use the handle end of a paintbrush to press 2 holes into each cupcake. Carefully press the straws into the holes. Finish by arranging 2 ice cream scoops, a scattering of ice cubes, and 1 fresh strawberry on each cupcake.

Candy straws

Juicy strawberry

Yummy ice cream

Soda shop favorite

Perfect when drunk with... ☞

Cheeseburger

Ingredients

- 1 quantity vanilla buttercream (see page 8)
- Red food coloring
- 5 cupcakes in yellow baking cups (see pages 6–7)
- 4$\frac{1}{2}$ oz (125 g) raisins
- 5 yellow fruit chews
- 5 mini cupcakes, baked with a generous sprinkling of sesame seeds (see page 7)
- 5 lengths of green chewy fruit roll
- 5 red thin, round gummy candies, about 1$\frac{1}{4}$ inches (3 cm) in diameter

Equipment

- Small sharp knife
- Small spatula
- Rolling pin
- Scissors

Preparing the cupcakes:
Reserve 2 tablespoons of the vanilla buttercream. Beat red food coloring into the remaining buttercream, adding a little at a time until the desired shade is reached. Cut the dome tops off each of the cupcakes to create a flat surface, and spread the buttercream over the cupcakes using a small spatula.

Burgers:
Put the raisins in a food processor and blend to a paste. (Alternatively, chop the raisins as finely as possible.) Divide the paste into 5 portions and pat each into a burger shape, moistening your hands with water if the raisin mixture is very sticky.

Melted cheese:
Soften the yellow fruit chews in the microwave for a few seconds if too firm to roll (see page 20). Roll out each fruit chew with a rolling pin until very thin. Trim off the edges with scissors, so the rolled chew measures about 2 inches (5 cm) across. Place one rolled fruit chew on top of each burger, bending the corners over the edges, for melted cheese.

Finishing touches:
Slice the mini cupcakes in half and position the bases on the cupcakes. Spread the bases with reserved vanilla buttercream. For each cupcake, scrunch up a length of chewy fruit roll and place toward one edge of the burger base. Top with a red gummy candy, a burger, and then the top half of the mini cupcake.

Other ideas: Spread extra cupcakes with buttercream in bright primary colors. Using a fluted fries cutter, cut $^1/_2$ inch (1 cm) slices from a densely textured Madeira cake, then cut the slices across into fries. Pile on top of the cupcakes.

Cool Dude

Ingredients

- Green food coloring
- 1 quantity glacé icing (see page 9)
- 5 cupcakes in blue baking cups (see pages 6–7)
- 3^1/$_2$ oz (100 g) white chocolate
- 2^3/$_4$ oz (75 g) semisweet or milk chocolate
- Tubes of black and red decorator frosting
- 2 strips of chewing gum
- 5 small candies

Equipment

- Small spatula
- Small sharp knife
- Paper pastry bag (see page 25)
- Scissors

Preparing the cakes: Beat green food coloring into the glacé icing, adding a little at a time until the desired shade is reached. Spread over the cupcakes using a small spatula.

Heads: Cut the white chocolate into 5 rectangles measuring about 2 x 1^3/$_4$ inches (5 x 4 cm). Press gently onto the cupcakes.

Facial features: Melt the semisweet or milk chocolate (see page 18). Let the chocolate cool slightly, then put into a paper pastry bag, snip off the merest tip and pipe hair around the top edges of each chocolate "head." Use black decorator frosting to pipe square sunglasses, noses, and eyebrows. Cut out ear shapes in chewing gum and tuck behind the white chocolate faces. Pipe outlines to the ears in red decorator frosting and then add a smiling mouth to each face.

Necklaces: Pipe a loop of red decorator frosting under each chin and secure a small candy in the center.

Other ideas: Create a whole family of funny faces by decorating each cupcake differently. Try different colored buttercream and types of chocolate, plus crazy hairstyles, ribbons and bows; freckles and beards; and different styles and pieces of jewelry.

YO DUUUUUUDDDDDDDDDDDDE!!

Stunning shades

Radical hair

Cartoon Bomb

Ingredients

- 5 cupcakes in red baking cups (see pages 6–7)
- 5 mini cupcakes (see page 7)
- 1 quantity vanilla buttercream (see page 8)
- 9 oz (250 g) fondant sugar
- Black food coloring
- 2 or 3 lengths of soft licorice
- 5 yellow or white birthday candles

Equipment

- Small spatula
- Small sharp knife

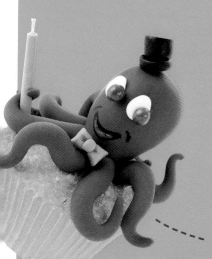

Preparing the cupcakes: Using a small spatula, spread a little vanilla buttercream over the larger cupcakes. Invert a mini cupcake onto the top of each, remove the baking cup, and round off the edges to create a dome shape. Spread the remaining buttercream over the domed tops. Once the cakes are covered, clean the spatula and dip it in hot water. Smooth out the buttercream with the warmed knife.

Bombs: Put the fondant sugar in a bowl and beat in a little water at a time until the liquid fondant thickly coats the back of the spoon. Beat in plenty of black food coloring. Hold a prepared cupcake over the bowl of liquid fondant and spoon the fondant over the buttercream, tilting the cupcake so the excess drips back into the bowl without running down the sides of the cupcake. Repeat with the 4 remaining cupcakes.

Lighters: Cut the licorice lengths into 1/2-inch (1-cm) pieces. Press a candle into the end of each piece of licorice and then push the licorice into the side of each cupcake until it feels secure. If it's difficult to push a candle through the center of the licorice, make a small incision with a sharp knife, then slot the candle in. After positioning the candles on the cupcakes, fill in any gaps around the licorice with leftover fondant.

Try me too! page 40

BOOOOOM!

BANG!

Make a wish

Explosive flavor!

Rubber Duck

Ingredients

- 4¹/₄ oz (125 g) marzipan
- 4¹/₄ oz (125 g) fondant sugar
- Yellow and blue food coloring
- Double quantity vanilla buttercream (see page 8)
- 5 cupcakes in yellow baking cups (see pages 6–7)
- 2 orange gummy candies
- Tube of black decorator frosting

Equipment

- Baking sheet
- Parchment paper
- Small spatula
- 2 paper pastry bags (see page 25)
- Scissors
- Small sharp knife

Rubber ducks: Lightly knead the marzipan to soften and divide into 5 pieces. Shape each into a chubby duck, pinching out a round head shape at one end and a pointed tail at the other. Put the fondant sugar in a bowl and beat in a little water at a time until the liquid fondant thickly coats the back of the spoon. Beat in yellow food coloring, adding a little at a time until the desired shade is reached. Coat one of the marzipan ducks in the fondant, then lift out on a wide-pronged fork, so the excess drips back into the bowl. Place on a baking sheet lined with parchment paper. Repeat for the remaining 4 ducks, then leave to harden for at least 2 hours.

Preparing the cupcakes: Beat blue food coloring into two-thirds of the vanilla buttercream, adding a little at a time until the desired pale blue shade is reached. Spread a little over the cupcakes using a small spatula.

Bubbles: Put the remaining blue buttercream in a paper pastry bag and the uncolored buttercream in another paper pastry bag. Snip off the tips of the bags so the buttercream can be piped in small blobs. Pipe pale blue blobs over the tops of the cupcakes. Perch a duck on top of each. Finish with patches of white bubbles.

Finishing touches: Use a small sharp knife to cut thin pieces of orange gummy candy. Secure 2 pieces on each duck with a little buttercream for beaks. Pipe round eyes with white buttercream and black decorator frosting in the centers.

QUACK!

QUACK!

QUACK!

QUACK!

Yummy duck

Splish splash!

Guess who's bathtime it is...

Resting Robot

Ingredients

- 5 cupcakes in black baking cups (see pages 6–7)
- 1 quantity vanilla buttercream (see page 8)
- Red or multicolored sprinkles
- 10 x 1$\frac{1}{4}$-inch (3-cm) lengths licorice sticks
- Small handful of white mini marshmallows
- 5$\frac{1}{4}$ oz (150 g) red rolled fondant
- Confectioners' sugar, for dusting
- 10 orange fruit chews
- Tubes of red and black decorator frosting
- 10 red candy-coated chocolates
- 2 strips of chewing gum

Equipment

- Small spatula
- Scissors

Preparing the cupcakes: Using a small spatula, spread the cupcakes with vanilla buttercream in a smooth layer and sprinkle with red or multicolored candy sprinkles.

Legs: Push 2 pieces of licorice onto the top of each cupcake for legs and then secure a marshmallow to one end of each for feet.

Bodies and heads: Divide the red fondant into 5 pieces. Using hands lightly dusted with confectioners' sugar, shape each piece into a rectangle. Press one rectangle gently onto the licorice at the opposite end to the marshmallow. Prop up with a piece of marshmallow. Press 2 orange fruit chews together until they stick. (If they don't stick, join them with decorator frosting.) Secure to the top of the red fondant with red decorator frosting. Repeat to give 5 robots.

Arms: Position a red candy-coated chocolate at either side of each body for the hands. Secure 2 or 3 marshmallows on top of each chocolate for arms, then pipe horizontal bands of red decorator frosting around the joins.

Finishing touches: Using scissors, cut 5 curved panels from the chewing gum and secure one to each rectangle with a dot of black decorator frosting. Pipe a simple design onto the front of each panel in decorator frosting. Cut out tiny strips from the chewing gum trimmings, pipe a line of red decorator frosting across the tops of the heads, and secure a row of chewing gum strips to each. Cut thin slices of marshmallow for ears and smaller pieces for eyes. Pipe a mouth onto each in red decorator frosting.

Toy Car

Ingredients

- 1 quantity vanilla buttercream (see page 8)
- 5 cupcakes in green baking cups (see pages 6–7)
- Black decorating sugar
- 7 oz (200 g) blue rolled fondant
- Confectioners' sugar, for dusting
- 10 decorating sugar pearls
- 5 flat chewy candies
- Tubes of black and yellow decorator frosting
- 20 mini red candy-covered chocolates
- Handful of jumbo snowflake-shaped sprinkles

Equipment

- Small spatula
- Scissors
- Small sharp knife

Preparing the cupcakes: Using a small spatula, spread vanilla buttercream over each cupcake as smoothly as possible, doming it slightly in the center.

Roads: Put the black decorating sugar on a plate and roll the tops of the cupcakes gently in the sugar until completely coated.

Cars: Divide the blue rolled fondant into 5 pieces and shape each into a car using hands lightly dusted with confectioners' sugar. The easiest way to do this is to shape a rectangular block, cut out a section at the front for the bonnet, and then smooth the edges. Rest each car on top of a cupcake. While the fondant is still soft, push 2 sugar pearls into the front of each car for headlights. For the windows, use scissors to cut out small rectangles from the flat chewy candy and press gently in position. (Secure with a little decorator frosting if they don't stay in place easily.) Pipe a line of black decorator frosting around each window and large blobs for wheels. Press a mini red candy-coated chocolate into the center of each wheel.

Finishing touches: Cut out ¼ x ⅛-inch (5 x 2.5-mm) strips from the flat chewy candy trimmings and press into the black decorating sugar for road markings. Secure a similarly sized piece of chewy candy to the front of each car for a license plate. Secure jumbo snowflake-shaped sprinkles around the edges of the cupcakes with dots of decorator frosting, then pipe yellow decorator frosting into the centers.

Try me too! page 36

Other ideas: Decorate plenty of cupcakes with roads and grass verges made by coloring shredded coconut with green food coloring (see page 22). Add flowers to each cupcake and then arrange them in a figure-of-eight, inserting the cars between them. If desired, make the fondant cars in a variety of different colors.

Golfer's Bag

Ingredients

- 13 oz (375 g) marzipan
- Confectioners' sugar, for dusting
- 10 chocolate-covered mint sticks
- $4^1/_2$ oz (125 g) fondant sugar
- Brown and green food coloring
- 5 cupcakes in green baking cups (see pages 6–7)
- 15 soft caramels
- 1 quantity vanilla buttercream (see page 8)
- 1 white fruit chew

Equipment

- Rolling pin
- Small spatula
- Paper pastry bag (see page 25)
- Scissors

Bags: Divide the marzipan into 5 pieces. On a surface lightly dusted with confectioners' sugar, shape each piece into a log shape measuring $2^1/_4$ inches (5.5 cm) long. Stand each log on one end to make sure it stands fairly upright. Use one of the chocolate-covered mint sticks to press 5 holes into the top of each log, ready to support the golf clubs. Put the fondant sugar in a bowl and beat in a little water at a time until the liquid fondant thickly coats the back of the spoon. Beat in brown food coloring, adding a little at a time until the desired shade is reached. Coat one of the marzipan logs in the fondant, then lift out on a wide-pronged fork, so the excess drips back into the bowl. Stand the log on one end on a cupcake. Repeat for the remaining 4 golf bags.

Clubs: Break the chocolate mint sticks into lengths between $^3/_4$ and $1^1/_2$ inches (2 and 3.5 cm) and push down into the tops of the "bags" so they're at varying heights. (You will need 5 sticks per cupcake.) Soften the caramels in the microwave for a few seconds if too firm to mold (see page 20). For each "club," mold pea-sized pieces of caramel into simple club-head shapes and rap around the ends of the "sticks." Roll out more softened caramel into 5 thin strips, measuring about $5^1/_2$ inches (13 cm) long, and wrap one strip around the top of each bag. Make 5 handles, measuring $1^1/_2$ x $^1/_2$ inch (3.5 x 1 cm), and press onto the sides of the bags.

Grass: Reserve 2 tablespoons of the vanilla buttercream. Beat green food coloring into the remaining buttercream, adding a little at a time until the desired shade is reached. Using a small spatula, spread the buttercream around the top edges of the cupcakes, peaking roughly to resemble grass.

Finishing touches: Put the reserved buttercream in a paper pastry bag and snip off the merest tip. Use to pipe stitching and pockets on the bags. Mold 5 tiny balls of caramel and press onto the pockets. Roll tiny pieces of fruit chew into small balls and scatter them on the grass.

Other ideas: Spread more cupcakes with buttercream in different shades of green or with crushed cookies to resemble sand. Scatter with golf balls, golf tees, or small red flags made from triangular pieces of red paper wrapped around the end of toothpicks.

Footballer's Boots

Ingredients

- 1 quantity white chocolate frosting (see page 10)
- 5 cupcakes in black baking cups (see pages 6–7)
- 2³/₄ oz (75 g) green decorating sugar (see page 22)
- 5¹/₄ oz (150 oz) white fruit chews
- Confectioners' sugar, for dusting
- 8-inch (20-cm) length of licorice wheel
- Tube of red decorator frosting
- 6-inch (15-cm) length of red sugar-coated licorice lace

Equipment

- Small spatula
- Small wooden spoon
- Small sharp knife

Grass: Using a small spatula, spread the white chocolate frosting over each cupcake as smoothly as possible, doming it generously in the center. Put the decorating sugar on a plate and roll the tops of the cupcakes in the sugar until completely coated.

Boots: For each pair of boots you'll need 1 oz (25 g) white fruit chews. Soften the fruit chews in the microwave for a few seconds if too firm to mold (see page 20). Divide the fruit chews in half and mold the pieces into log shapes with rounded ends. Dip the handle end of a wooden spoon into a little confectioners' sugar to stop it sticking and then press it into one end of the log shapes to form the "boot." Repeat to give 10 boots.

To decorate the boots, cut off rectangles of licorice measuring 1 x ¹/₂ inch (2.5 x 1 cm). Slice off the corners at one end, cut almost in half lengthwise, and secure to the boots. Press a pair of boots gently onto each cupcake. Pipe markings on the sides and openings of the boots in red decorator frosting.

Laces: Pipe criss-cross laces over the licorice in red decorator frosting. Cut 10 lengths of red licorice lace and secure 2 to each boot with decorator frosting. Let the ends trail over the "grass."

Other ideas: Spread more cupcakes with grass and decorate with foil-wrapped chocolate footballs, scarfs made from rolled fondant in team colors, and red and yellow cards made from molded fruit chews.

Try me too! page 122

GOAL!

GOAL!

Winning laces

Go team!

Game time

Turn over for more playtime fun! 👉

Pretty Ballerina

Ingredients

- 1 quantity vanilla buttercream (see page 8)
- 5 cupcakes in pink baking cups (see pages 6–7)
- 7 oz (200 g) white rolled fondant
- Confectioners' sugar, for dusting
- 9 oz (250 g) flesh-colored rolled fondant
- Yellow, brown, and red food colorings
- 5 pink or red candy-coated chocolates
- 5 x 4-inch (10-cm) lengths of red sugar-coated licorice lace
- Tube of white decorator frosting
- 5 heart-shaped decorating sprinkles

Equipment

- Small spatula
- Rolling pin
- 3-inch (7-cm) and 1^1/$_2$-inch (3.5-cm) round cookie cutter
- Toothpicks
- Fine paintbrush
- Parchment paper
- Paper pastry bag (see page 25)

Preparing the cupcakes: Reserve 2 tablespoons of the vanilla buttercream, then spread the remainder over the cupcakes using a small spatula.

Tutus: For each cupcake, roll out one-fifth of the white rolled fondant on a surface dusted with confectioners' sugar until about ^{1}/$_{16}$ inch (2 mm) thick. Cut out one disk using a 3-inch (7-cm) cookie cutter, then cut out the center using a 1^1/$_2$-inch (3.5-cm) cookie cutter. Cut the ring of fondant in half. Roll a horizontally held toothpick around the outer edge of one half of the fondant so that it starts to frill (see page 14). Secure the frill around the top edge of the cupcake, then shape and secure the second frill. Repeat so there are 3 frills on each of the cupcakes.

Bodies: For each body, take a 1-oz (25-g) piece of flesh-colored fondant and roll into an oval shape. Dampen the inner edges of the white icing using a dampened paintbrush and position the oval on the center of one cupcake. Trace the bodice template (see page 126) onto parchment paper and cut out. Roll out the remaining white fondant until about ^{1}/$_{16}$ inch (2 mm) thick and cut around the template using a small sharp knife. Secure to the front of the body using a dampened paintbrush. Cover the back with a rectangle of fondant. Repeat to give 5 bodies.

Arms and heads: To shape each pair of arms, take a ^{1}/$_4$-oz (5-g) piece of flesh-colored fondant and roll into 2^1/$_2$-inch (6-cm) lengths slightly tapered at the ends. Cut in half and push half a toothpick through the thick ends. Attach the arms to the body, pressing them horizontally into the shoulder area. Flatten the tapered ends slightly to shape hands. For the heads, roll 5 cherry-sized balls of flesh-colored fondant and secure to the bodies.

Hair: Beat yellow food coloring into the reserved buttercream, adding a little at a time until the desired shade is reached. Put the buttercream in a paper pastry bag and snip off the merest tip. Use to pipe hair on each head. Press a candy-coated chocolate on top of the hair and pipe more buttercream on top.

Faces: Paint on eyes and noses using a fine paintbrush and brown food coloring and mouths in red food coloring.

Jewelry: Wrap a licorice lace around each waist, securing at the back with a little white decorator frosting. Pipe a necklace and bracelet on each ballerina in decorator frosting. Secure a heart-shaped decorating sprinkle to each necklace.

Dressing up

Ingredients

- 4$\frac{1}{2}$ oz (125 g) fondant sugar
- Pink food coloring
- 5 cupcakes in purple baking cups (see pages 6–7)
- 25 pink fruit chews
- 8-inch (20-cm) length of licorice wheel
- Tube of black decorator frosting
- 5 pink dragées
- Ribbon (optional)

Equipment

- Small spatula
- Small sharp knife

Preparing the cupcakes: Put the fondant sugar in a bowl and beat in a little water at a time until the liquid fondant holds its shape briefly when the spoon is lifted from the bowl. Beat in pink food coloring, adding a little at a time until the desired shade is reached. Using a small spatula, spread the fondant over the tops of the cupcakes, letting it run down the sides slightly.

Handbags: Take 2 pink fruit chews and soften in the microwave for a few seconds if too firm to mold (see page 20). Shape into a block, then pinch the top edge together. Cut a very thin strip from the length of licorice wheel and then cut the strip into 2-inch (5-cm) lengths. Secure the ends of one piece to both ends of the handbag with black decorator frosting to shape a handle. Pipe a line of decorator frosting along the top of the handbag and press a sugar pink dragée in the center for the handbag clasp. Make 4 more handbags in the same way, then position one on each cupcake.

Shoes: For each shoe, slice off a thin piece of a pink fruit chew and roll under your finger to shape a high heel. Mold the remaining piece of fruit chew into a rectangle about 1$\frac{1}{4}$ inches (3 cm) long. Bend at both ends to create an arc shape. Attach the heel to one end of the arc and then position the shoe on the cupcake. Repeat to give 10 shoes. Cut 10 fine strips of licorice, measuring about 1$\frac{1}{4}$ inches (3 cm). Bend each into a loop and secure at the heels of the shoes with dots of black decorator frosting. Pipe straps of decorator frosting across the fronts of the shoes.

Finishing touches: If using ribbon, secure lengths around the sides of the cakes with black decorator frosting.

So pretty!

Fancy footwork

Fabulous fashion

Be My Valentine

Ingredients

- 5¼ oz (150 g) red hard candies
- A little vegetable oil
- 1 quantity white chocolate frosting (see page 10)
- 5 cupcakes in pink baking cups (see pages 6–7)
- Tube of red decorator frosting
- Red decorating sugar (see page 22)

Equipment

- Baking sheet
- Parchment paper
- Metal heart-shaped cookie cutters in 3 different sizes, measuring between 1¼ and 2 inches (3 and 5 cm) from point to point
- Plastic wrap
- Large pastry bag
- ½-inch (1-cm) star pastry tip

Hearts: Line a baking sheet with parchment paper and preheat the oven to 400°F (200°C). Unwrap the red hard candies and space them 2 inches (5 cm) apart on the paper. Cook for about 5 minutes, watching closely, until the sweets have melted and spread over the paper in a syrupy layer. While melting, dip the edges of the 3 heart-shaped cookie cutters in a little oil. Remove the sweets from the oven and cool for 30 seconds. Working quickly, press the cutters firmly into the melted candy making as many hearts as you can before the syrup sets. Let cool until brittle, then peel back the paper and gently snap the heart shapes free. Remelt the candy trimmings and use to shape more hearts. (You'll need a total of 15 hearts, 5 of each size.) If you're not decorating the cupcakes immediately, sandwich the hearts between sheets of oiled plastic wrap to prevent them turning sticky.

Preparing the cupcakes: Put the white chocolate frosting into a large pastry bag fitted with a star pastry tip, then pipe generous swirls of frosting over the cupcakes.

Finishing touches: Use red decorator frosting to pipe an outline around each heart, then carefully press one heart in each size into the frosting on each cupcake. Sprinkle red decorating sugar over the frosting on each cake.

True love

Romance is in the air!

Pretty Parcel

Ingredients

- 6 oz (175 g) fondant sugar
- Brown and blue food coloring
- 5 cupcakes in blue baking cups (see pages 6–7)
- 3¹/₄ yd (3 m) lightweight blue and brown patterned ribbon, about ¹/₂ inch (1 cm) wide

Equipment

- 2 paper pastry bags (see page 25)
- Scissors
- Small spatula

Preparing the cupcakes: Put the fondant sugar in a bowl and beat in a little water at a time until the liquid fondant thickly coats the back of the spoon. Spoon 2 tablespoons into a separate bowl and beat in brown food coloring, adding a little at a time until the desired shade is reached. Put in a paper pastry bag and snip off the merest tip. Color the remaining fondant blue using the same technique. Using a small spatula, spread the blue fondant over the cupcakes in a smooth layer. While the fondant is still soft, pipe dots of brown fondant all over the surface of the cakes and leave for several hours or overnight to set. (Reserve a little blue fondant for securing the ribbons.)

Ribbon: Put the reserved fondant in a paper pastry bag and snip off the merest tip. For each cupcake, cut two 8-inch (20-cm) lengths of ribbon. Wrap one length over the top of the cupcake and secure underneath with a dot of icing. Wrap the other length in the opposite direction and secure underneath. Repeat with the remaining 4 cupcakes. Make 5 small bows from the remaining ribbon and secure to the tops of the cupcakes.

Try me too! page 44

Other ideas: Decorate parcel cupcakes in various other colors and designs, such as stripes or simple flowers. Buy the ribbon before you start, so you can make the fondant in colors that complement the ribbon.

Wedding Cake

Ingredients

- 1 quantity royal icing (see page 9)
- Pink food coloring
- 5 cupcakes in pink baking cups (see pages 6–7)
- 5 teaspoons raspberry jelly
- Plenty of mini marshmallows
- 2 white fruit chews
- Silver dragées

Equipment

- Small sharp knife
- Teaspoon
- Small spatula
- 2 paper pastry bags (see page 25)
- Scissors
- Rolling pin
- Small heart-shaped cookie cutter, measuring about 1/2 inch (1 cm) from point to point

Preparing the cupcakes: Reserve 4 tablespoons of the royal icing. Beat pink food coloring into the remaining royal icing, adding a little at a time until a deep pink shade is reached. Cut the dome top off each cupcake to create a flat surface. Spread the raspberry jelly over the cupcakes with the back of a teaspoon, then spoon the pink royal icing on top. Using a small spatula, level the icing as smoothly as possible so that no cake shows through.

Wedding cakes: Spoon half the reserved royal icing into a paper pastry bag and snip off the merest tip. Arrange a circle of mini marshmallows over the top of one cupcake so the diameter is about 2 inches (5 cm). Press more marsmallows into the center, holding them all in place by piping the icing into the gaps. Arrange another layer of marshmallows on top to create a middle tier, making the diameter about $1^3/_4$ inches (4 cm). Finally, arrange 3 marshmallows on top. Repeat with the 4 remaining cupcakes.

Finishing touches: Soften the fruit chews in the microwave for a few seconds if too firm to roll (see page 20). Roll out thinly and cut out heart shapes with the cookie cutter. Secure to the tops of the wedding cakes with a little piped icing. Beat pink food coloring into the remaining icing, adding a little at a time until a pale pink shade is reached. Put in a paper pastry bag and snip off the merest tip. Use to pipe a scalloped edge around the cake tiers. Push a silver dragée into each point.

Love is sweet

Beautiful layers

Delightful dragées

Tea Party

Ingredients

- 5 cupcakes in pink or white baking cups (see pages 6–7)
- 5 teaspoons raspberry or strawberry jelly
- 5 thin cookies, about 3 inches (7 cm) in diameter
- $1/2$ quantity vanilla buttercream (see page 8)
- 9 oz (250 g) pink rolled fondant
- Confectioners' sugar, for dusting
- 5 red or pink round fruit chews
- Multicolored sprinkles
- 5 thin, round gummy candies, about 1 inch (2.5 cm) in diameter
- Tubes of white and red decorator frosting
- $2^3/4$ oz (75 g) white rolled fondant
- 10 heart-shaped candies

Equipment

- Small sharp knife
- Small spatula
- Rolling pin
- Fine paintbrush
- Pen

Preparing the cupcakes: Cut the dome top off each cupcake to create a flat surface. Using a small spatula, spread each cupcake with a little jelly and press a cookie down gently on top. Spread a thin layer of vanilla buttercream over each cookie.

Tablecloths: Divide the pink fondant into 5 pieces. For each cupcake, roll a piece of fondant on a surface lightly dusted with confectioners' sugar until about $1/16$ inch (2 mm) thick. Cut out a 4-inch (10-cm) square. Position the square over the cookie, so the fondant drapes down the sides. Use your fingers to make small folds along the edge of the tablecloth.

Sandwich cakes: Cut the round fruit chews in half and sandwich with a little buttercream. Spread a little more buttercream over the top of each "cake," then press it gently into the multicolored sprinkles. Secure to a thin, round gummy candy with a little white decorator frosting and secure the cake to the tablecloth with more frosting. Repeat to give 5 "cakes."

Teapots: For each teapot, roll a cherry-sized ball of white fondant under your fingertips and then lengthen slightly into an oval shape. Press a flattened ball of fondant onto the top for a lid, securing in place with a dampened paintbrush. Shape a small handle and spout and secure in place, then secure each teapot to a tablecloth using a dampened paintbrush.

Teacups: Roll 10 pea-sized pieces of white fondant in balls and press over the end of a pen to shape as cups. Secure onto 10 flattened balls of white fondant, as saucers. Pipe handles in white decorator frosting. Secure 2 cups to each tablecloth with a dampened paintbrush.

Finishing touches: Use red decorator frosting to pipe a decorative edge around each tablecloth, decorative dots on the teapots, and to create lid handles. Secure 2 heart-shaped candies to each tablecloth with decorator frosting.

Big Surf

Ingredients

- 1³/₄ oz (50 g) flesh-colored rolled fondant
- Confectioners' sugar, for dusting
- 1³/₄ oz (50 g) yellow rolled fondant
- Blue food coloring
- ¹/₂ quantity vanilla buttercream (see page 8)
- 5 cupcakes in white baking cups (see pages 6–7)
- 3¹/₂ oz (100 g) white rolled fondant
- Small piece of orange rolled fondant
- Red and green icing pens

Equipment

- Small sharp knife
- Baking sheet
- Parchment paper
- Scissors
- Rolling pin
- Small spatula

Legs: Divide the flesh-colored fondant into 10 pieces. Roll each piece into a sausage shape on a surface lightly dusted with confectioners' sugar, making one end slightly thinner. Bend the thinner ends over and flatten slightly to shape feet. Indent toes with the tip off a small sharp knife, then carefully place the "legs" on a baking sheet lined with parchment paper.

Surfboards: Trace the surfboard template (see page 127) onto parchment paper and cut out. Roll out the yellow fondant until about ¹/₈ inch (2.5 mm) thick and cut around the template. Repeat to give 5 shapes. Transfer to the baking sheet and leave to harden with the legs for at least 3 hours or overnight.

Preparing the cupcakes: Beat blue food coloring into the vanilla buttercream, adding a little at a time until the desired shade is reached. Using a small spatula, spread buttercream over each cupcake as smoothly as possible, doming it slightly in the center. Press the legs gently down into the buttercream.

Waves: Trace wave templates (see page 127) onto parchment paper and cut out. Roll out the white fondant until about ¹/₁₀ inch (2.5 mm) thick and cut around the templates. Repeat until you have 5 sets of "waves." Arrange each set of waves around the legs on the cupcakes, curving the pieces so they fall over the sides. If necessary, prop up the fondant with pieces of paper towel to hold the shapes until they harden. From the fondant trimmings, cut out small teardrop shapes. Secure several shapes to the baking cups of each cupcake with buttercream.

Shorts: Thinly roll out the orange fondant and cut out 10 strips, each measuring about 2 x ¹/₂ inches (5 x 1 cm). Wrap a strip around the top of each of the legs.

Finishing touches: Using red and green icing pens, put spots on the shorts and a decorative design on the surfboards. Gently press the surfboards in place on the cupcakes. (If they start to topple backward, prop them up with toothpicks.)

Sandcastle

Ingredients

- Double quantity vanilla buttercream (see page 8)
- 5 cupcakes in blue baking cups (see pages 6–7)
- 5 mini cupcakes (see page 7)
- 4 graham crackers, crushed
- 2 licorice chews
- 5 orange fruit chews
- Several lengths of green chewy fruit rolls
- 5 sandwich flags

Equipment

- Small spatula
- Small sharp knife
- Rolling pin
- Star cookie cutter, measuring about 1 inch (2.5 cm) from point to point

Preparing the cupcakes: Using a small spatula, spread a generous layer of buttercream over each larger cupcake, doming it up in the center. Invert the mini cupcakes onto the work surface, remove the baking cups, and slice off the edges to make sandcastle shapes. Position one mini cupcake on each cupcake, then cover with a generous layer of buttercream.

Sandcastles: Press the graham cracker crumbs all over the buttercream in a thick layer. (Try and flatten the crumbs on the "sandcastle" so it looks molded.) Cut small pieces from a licorice chew and press into the sandcastle to form an archway. Repeat to give 5 sandcastles.

Finishing touches: Soften the orange fruit chews in the microwave for a few seconds if too firm to roll (see page 20). Roll out thinly and cut out 5 star shapes using the cookie cutter. Position a star shape on each cupcake. Cut the green chewy fruit roll into thin strips and scrunch up around the edges of the sandcastles. Press a sandwich flag into the top of each cupcake.

Try me too! page 110

A beach adventure

Top of the castle

Candy starfish

Guess who is ready to play...

Jolly Clown

Ingredients

- Red food coloring
- 1 quantity vanilla buttercream (see page 8)
- 5 cupcakes in yellow baking cups (see pages 6–7)
- 5 mini cupcakes (see page 7)
- Mini red and yellow candy-coated chocolates
- 2 licorice wheels
- Tubes of yellow, red, and black decorator frosting
- 2³/₄ oz (75 g) orange rolled fondant
- Confectioners' sugar, for dusting
- 5 large white marshmallows
- 5 red gummy candy drops

Equipment

- Small sharp knife
- Small spatula
- Rolling pin
- 3-inch (7-cm) round cookie cutter
- 1¹/₂-inch (3.5-cm) round cookie cutter
- Toothpick

Preparing the cupcakes: Beat red food coloring into the vanilla buttercream, adding a little at a time until the desired shade is reached. Cut the dome tops off each of the cupcakes. Using a small spatula, spread a little buttercream over the larger cupcakes. Invert a mini cupcake onto the top of each, remove the baking cup, and round off the edges to create a dome shape. Spread more buttercream over each of the cupcakes in an even layer. Once they are all covered, clean the spatula and dip it in hot water. Smooth out the buttercream with the warmed knife.

Clown suits: Position 3 candy-covered chocolates down the front of each cupcake for buttons. Cut the licorice into 10 lengths measuring 3¹/₂ inches (9 cm), and secure 2 lengths to each cupcake for braces. Pipe a dot of yellow decorator frosting at the ends of each brace.

Frilly collars: Divide the orange fondant into 5 pieces. For each cupcake, roll out one piece of orange rolled fondant on a surface dusted with confectioners' sugar until about ¹/₁₆ inch (2 mm) thick. Cut out one disk using a 3-inch (7-cm) cookie cutter and then cut out the center using a 1¹/₂-inch (3.5-cm) cookie cutter. Cut the ring of fondant in half. Roll a horizontally held toothpick around the outer edge of one half of the fondant so that it starts to frill (see page 14). Secure the frill around the top of the clown suit, then shape and secure the second frill. Repeat for the remaining 4 clown suits.

Faces and hair: For each clown, position a marshmallow on top of the frills, securing with a little red decorator frosting. Secure a red candy-covered chocolate to the center of the marshmallow for a nose. Pipe a large mouth on each face in red decorator frosting and 2 small crosses in black decorator frosting for eyes. For the hair, pipe plenty of yellow decorator frosting. Push a red gummy candy drop onto the hair and then pipe a blob of black decorating frosting on top.

Other ideas: Spread additional cupcakes with buttercream colored red, yellow, and orange. Press contrasting candy-coated chocolates onto some of the cupcakes to give a spotty effect, and scatter others with juggling balls, skittles, or balloons molded out of rolled fondant.

Fairy

Ingredients

- 1 quantity vanilla buttercream (see page 8)
- 5 cupcakes in yellow baking cups (see pages 6–7)
- Pearlized multicolor sprinkles
- 5 ice cream cones
- $1^3/_4$ oz (50 g) pale pink rolled fondant
- Confectioners' sugar, for dusting
- 5 pink decorating sugar pearls (or small, round candies)
- Yellow and brown food coloring
- 2 yellow fruit chews
- 2 sheets rice paper

Equipment

- Small spatula
- Serrated knife
- 5 pink baking cups
- Scissors
- Adhesive tape
- Fine paintbrush
- Paper pastry bag (see page 25)
- Small sharp knife
- Parchment paper

Preparing the cupcakes: Reserve 2 tablespoons of the vanilla buttercream, then spread the remainder over the cupcakes using a small spatula. Put the pearlized multicolor sprinkles on a plate and press the tops of the cakes gently into the sprinkles until completely covered.

Dresses and arms: Using a serrated knife, cut the ice cream cones down to $2^1/_2$-inch (6-cm) lengths and press the inverted cones gently onto the tops of the cupcakes. For each cupcake, take an almond-sized piece of pink rolled fondant and, about $^1/_2$ inch (1 cm) down from the cone tip, wrap the fondant around the cone, pressing gently to secure. Cut the fluted area of a pink baking cup away from the flat base with scissors, then wrap around the cone beneath the fondant. (You'll need about half a case for each dress.) Secure at the back with adhesive tape.

On a surface dusted with confectioners' sugar, roll a little pink fondant under your fingers into a very thin sausage shape measuring about $1^3/_4$ inches (4 cm) long. Cut in half and secure the arms to the bodies of the cupcake using a dampened paintbrush. Bend the ends slightly for hands. Secure a decorating sugar pearl to the front of the dress with a little buttercream. Repeat with the remaining 4 cupcakes.

Faces, hair, and crowns: Roll 5 cherry-sized balls of fondant for heads. Press gently in place. Beat yellow food coloring into the reserved buttercream, adding a little at a time until the desired shade is reached. Put in a paper pastry bag, snip off the merest tip, and pipe hair on each of the heads. Use a paintbrush and brown food coloring to paint facial features on each fairy. Using a small sharp knife, cut thin slices from the yellow fruit chews and shape into crowns. Gently press the crowns into the hair.

Wings: Trace the wing template (see opposite) onto parchment paper and cut out. Cut out 5 sets of wings in rice paper using the template as a guide. Secure to the backs of the fairies with buttercream.

Other ideas: Decorate additional cupcakes with pearlized multicolor sprinkles as above. Scatter with candy stars or stars cut out of rolled fondant in pastel colors. Cut strips of flat chewy candies for wands and secure small star sprinkles to the ends.

Sugar Monster

Ingredients

- 5 cupcakes in yellow baking cups (see pages 6–7)
- 5 mini cupcakes
- 1 quantity vanilla buttercream (see page 8)
- Pink decorating sugar (see page 22)
- 2 large white marshmallows
- Tube of yellow decorator frosting
- 10 small square candies
- 10 mini yellow candy-coated chocolates
- 10 small, flat green gummy candies
- 5 large, flat yellow gummy candies

Equipment

- Small sharp knife
- Small spatula

Preparing the cupcakes: Cut the dome tops off each of the cupcakes. Using a small spatula, spread a little vanilla buttercream over the larger cupcakes. Invert a mini cupcake onto the top of each, remove the baking cup, and round off the edges to create a dome shape. Spread more buttercream over each of the cupcakes in an even layer. Once they are all covered, clean the spatula and dip it in hot water. Smooth out the buttercream with the warmed knife. Put the decorating sugar on a plate, then press the surfaces of the cupcakes gently into the sugar until completely coated.

Faces: Cut 3 thin slices from each of the marshmallows and then cut the slices in half to make semicircular shapes. For each monster, press a piece of marshmallow into the colored sugar to shape a mouth. Secure with decorator frosting if the marshmallow doesn't stay in place. Push the square candies into the sugar for eyes, securing mini candy-coated chocolates in the centers with decorator frosting. Cut 5 of the small green gummy candies in half and position for eyebrows.

Finishing touches: Make deep cuts into the 5 large, flat yellow gummy candies and open out to shape hair. Press gently into the tops of the cupcakes. Cut the remaining green gummy candies in half and secure to the bases of the cupcakes with decorator frosting for feet. Pipe an outline around the marshmallow mouths with the decorator frosting.

Other ideas: Use decorating sugar in different colors and an assortment of gummy candies of various sizes and shapes.

Chewy monster hair

Sugar head

Don't eat me
before bed!

Monster feet

Easter Bunny

Ingredients

- 3¹/₂ oz (100 g) white chocolate, chopped
- Mini marshmallows
- 2 candied cherries
- 1 oz (25 g) semisweet or milk chocolate, chopped
- Green food coloring
- 1 quantity vanilla buttercream (see page 8)
- 5 cupcakes in pink or green baking cups (see pages 6–7)
- Small jelly beans

Equipment

- Parchment paper
- 2 paper pastry bags (see page 25)
- Scissors
- 5 craft or popsicle sticks
- Toothpick
- Small sharp knife
- Small spatula
- Large pastry bag
- Small star pastry tip

Bunnies: Trace the bunny template (see page 126) onto parchment paper. Lay a second larger sheet of parchment paper over the traced outline. Melt the white chocolate (see page 18), then put into a paper pastry bag and snip off the merest tip. Pipe a thin line of chocolate around the edge of the bunny shape. Slide the top sheet of parchment over a little so you can pipe more shapes. (You'll need 5 in total, but it's worth making a couple extra in case of breakages.) Once all the outlines are done, place a craft or popsicle stick at the base of the shape so half the stick is in the body area of the bunny (see page 19). Snip off a little more of the paper pastry bag and fill in the centers of the bunny shapes, spreading the chocolate into the corners with a toothpick and covering the sticks as you go.

Faces: Cut thin slices of marshmallow and position on each bunny for eyes. Cut out small triangles of candied cherries and position for noses. Melt the semisweet chocolate and put in a paper pastry bag. Snip off the merest tip and use to pipe outlines of the ears, the centers of the eyes, smiling mouths, and little dots on the cheeks. Cut rectangles from a marshmallow, as small as you can, and position for teeth. Leave to harden in a cool place or refrigerate for at least 1 hour.

Preparing the cupcakes: Beat green food coloring into the buttercream, adding a little at a time until the desired shade is reached. Spread a little over each cupcake with a small spatula, doming it up slightly in the center. Put the remainder in a pastry bag fitted with a star pastry tip and use to pipe stars all over the buttercream.

Assembling: Carefully peel the parchment paper away from the bunny shapes and push one into each cupcake. Press plenty of small jelly beans into the green buttercream.

Santa Claus

Ingredients

- 7 oz (200 g) royal icing sugar
- 5 cupcakes in white baking cups (see pages 6–7)
- 30 orange fruit chews
- 12 pink fruit chews
- 4¹/₂ oz (125 g) red rolled fondant
- Confectioners' sugar, for dusting
- Tubes of white, black, and red decorator frosting
- Black food coloring
- Snowflake sprinkles

Equipment

- Small sharp knife
- Fine paintbrush

Snow: Put the royal icing sugar in a bowl and beat in enough water to make a thick paste that doesn't quite hold its shape. Spoon the icing over each cupcake, spreading it to the edges and letting it run down the sides slightly.

Chimneys: Cut the orange fruit chews in half. Arrange 6 pieces in a square on the icing on each cupcake. Arrange another 6 slices on top to resemble a chimney. If necessary, secure in place with dots of royal icing. Place a pink fruit chew in the center of each chimney.

Santas: To make each Santa's body, take a ¹/₂-oz (15-g) ball of red rolled fondant and flatten slightly on a surface dusted with confectioners' sugar. Position each body on top of a chimney. For the faces, soften 5 pink fruit chews in the microwave for a few seconds if too firm to mold (see page 20). Squeeze each into a round shape and position on top of a body.

For each pair of arms, roll a little red fondant into a sausage shape about 1³/₄ inches (4 cm) long and tapered slightly at the ends. Make a diagonal cut through the center and position the pieces on either side of the body. Secure in place with a dampened paintbrush.

Soften the remaining pink fruit chews, then pull off pea-sized balls and shape into hands. Use a small sharp knife to indent fingers and thumbs on the hands. Secure in place with dots of white decorator frosting. Shape more red fondant into Santa hats and secure in place with decorator frosting.

Try me too! page 112

Finishing touches:

Use the white, black, and red decorator frosting to pipe the trim on the hats, beards, buttons on the jackets, and each nose and mouth. Use a paintbrush and black food coloring to paint downward-looking eyes. Arrange snowflake sprinkles over the cakes, securing with dots of white decorator frosting.

Christmas Tree

Ingredients

- 5 cupcakes in red baking cups (see pages 6–7)
- 1 tablespoon apricot jelly
- 2³/₄ oz (75 g) marzipan
- 1 quantity royal icing (see page 9)
- 5 ice cream cones
- Red and green food coloring
- Green or silver dragées
- White decorating sugar pearls (or small, round candies)
- 2 white fruit chews

Equipment

- Serrated knife
- Teaspoon
- Small spatula
- 2 paper pastry bags (see page 25)
- Small star pastry tip
- Rolling pin
- Small star cutter, measuring about ³/₄ inch (2 cm) from point to point

Preparing the cupcakes: Cut the dome top off each cupcake to create a flat surface. Spread the apricot jelly over the cupcakes with the back of a teaspoon. Divide the marzipan into 5 pieces, then roll each into a ball and press flat. Press gently into the cupcake centers. Using a small spatula, spread a little royal icing over the cupcakes as smoothly as possible so that no cake shows through.

Trees: Measure 2 inches (5 cm) from the tip of the cones and slice off the excess with a serrated knife. Press an inverted cone gently into the top of each cupcake. Beat red food coloring into 2 tablespoons of royal icing, adding a little at a time until the desired shade is reached. Put in a paper pastry bag and snip off the merest tip. Color the remaining royal icing with green food coloring using the same technique. Fit another paper pastry bag with the star pastry tip and fill with the green icing. Starting at the base of each ice cream cone, pipe rows of green stars onto the cones. To do this, pipe a star and then pull away the bag as you stop squeezing out the icing. Continue until you complete one row and then add further rows until the whole cone is covered.

Decorations: While the green royal icing is still soft, pipe curved lines of red icing around the trees. Gently push the dragées and decorating sugar pearls into the icing at regular intervals. Soften the fruit chews in the microwave for a few seconds if too firm to roll (see page 20). Roll out thinly and cut out star shapes using the small cutter. Secure to the tops of the trees.

Other ideas: To create a colorful platter of Chrismas cakes, decorate additional cupcakes with royal icing, dragées, decorating sugar pearls, and fruit-chew stars of different colors. You can also make small presents to arrange around the trees by piping royal icing as ribbon around small, colorful hard candies.

Sleighbells

Ingredients

- 5 cupcakes in black baking cups (see pages 6–7)
- 5 mini cupcakes (see page 7)
- 1 quantity vanilla buttercream (see page 8)
- Dark blue food coloring
- Edible gold or silver star sprinkles
- 2³/₄ oz (75 g) white chocolate, chopped
- 5 deep pink fruit chews
- 5 orange fruit chews

Equipment

- Small sharp knife
- Small spatula
- Parchment paper
- Paper pastry bag (see page 25)
- Scissors
- Toothpick

Night sky: Cut the dome tops off each of the cupcakes. Spread a little vanilla buttercream over the larger cupcakes and invert a mini cupcake onto the top of each. Remove the baking cups, then use a sharp knife to round off the edges to create a smooth, rounded top. Beat dark blue food coloring into the remaining buttercream, adding a little at a time until the desired shade is reached. Using a small spatula, spread the buttercream over each domed cupcake. Once the cakes are covered, clean the spatula and dip in hot water. Smooth out the buttercream with the warmed knife. Scatter with edible gold or silver star sprinkles.

Sleighs: Trace the sleigh template (see page 127) onto parchment paper. Lay a second larger sheet of parchment paper over the traced outline. Melt the chocolate (see page 18), then put in a paper pastry bag and snip off the merest tip. Pipe a thin line of chocolate around the edge of the sleigh shape. Slide the top sheet of parchment over a little so you can pipe more shapes. (You'll need 5 in total, but it's worth making a couple extra in case of breakages.) Once all the outlines are done, fill in the centers, spreading the chocolate into the corners with a toothpick. Leave the shapes to harden in a cool place or refrigerate for at least 1 hour.

Villages: Cut the fruit chews into thin slices and then cut out small house shapes, each with a pointed roof. Press into the buttercream around one side of each cupcake. Pipe a little white chocolate over each roof.

Finishing touches: Carefully peel the parchment paper away from the sleigh shapes and gently press them into the tops of the cupcakes.

Sparkly stars

Head for the chimney

Sugar town

Turn over for more festive fun! ☞

Snowman

Ingredients

- 5 cupcakes in white baking cups (see pages 6–7)
- 5 mini cupcakes (see page 7)
- 9 oz (250 g) fondant sugar
- 1 quantity vanilla buttercream (see page 8)
- 5 large marshmallows
- 5 flat, round gummy candies, about 1¼ inches (3 cm) in diameter
- 5 pink decorating sugar pearls (or small, round candies)
- Sugar-coated, multicolored chewy fruit rolls
- Handful of currants
- 2 orange gummy candies

Equipment

- Small sharp knife
- Small spatula

Snowmen: Cut the dome top off each cupcake to create a flat surface. Put the fondant sugar in a bowl and beat in a little water at a time until the liquid fondant thickly coats the back of the spoon. Using a small spatula, spread a little buttercream over the larger cupcakes. Invert a mini cupcake onto the top of each, remove the baking cups, then spread the buttercream evenly over each mini cupcake. Hold a prepared cupcake over the bowl of liquid fondant and spoon the fondant over the buttercream, tilting the cupcake so the excess drips back into the bowl without running down the sides of the cupcake. Repeat with the remaining 4 cupcakes. To make the heads, coat the large marshmallows in fondant and position one on top of each cupcake.

Hats and scarfs: Press a flat, round gummy candy onto the top of each cupcake, then secure a small decorating sugar pearl or small, round candy to each center with a little fondant. Cut 5 lengths of the multicolored chewy fruit rolls and secure around the necks for scarfs. Cut 10 shorter lengths and secure 2 to the front of each scarf.

Finishing touches: Press currants into the fondant for eyes and buttons while it is still soft. Secure more currants to the front of each baking cup with a little leftover fondant for buttons. Cut more currants into pieces and position for mouths. Use a small sharp knife to shape 5 noses out of the 2 orange gummy candies, then position on each face.

Try me too! page 30

Pointy carrot nose

All wrapped up

Dashing cool buttons

Guess who's too hot for comfort...

Dragon

Ingredients

- 5 cupcakes in purple baking cups (see pages 6–7)
- 5 teaspoons raspberry or strawberry jelly
- 2¾ oz (75 g) lilac rolled fondant
- Confectioners' sugar, for dusting
- 8 oz (225 g) green rolled fondant
- 3 Oreo™ cookies
- Tube of green and red decorator frosting
- 8-inch (20-cm) length red chewy fruit roll
- Small piece white rolled fondant
- Green food coloring or icing pen

Equipment

- Rolling pin
- 3-inch (7-cm) round cookie cutter
- Small sharp knife
- Fine paintbrush
- ¾-inch (2-cm) round cookie cutter

Preparing the cupcakes: Spread each cupcake with a little jelly. Roll out the lilac rolled fondant on a surface lightly dusted with confectioners' sugar until about $^1/_{16}$ inch (2 mm) thick, then cut out 5 disks using a 3-inch (7-cm) round cookie cutter. (You'll need to reroll the trimmings to make enough disks.) Position a disk over each cupcake, gently easing the fondant to fit around the sides. Trim off any excess fondant around the edges of the cups.

Dragons: Reserve $^1/_2$ oz (15 g) of the green rolled fondant and divide the remainder into 5 pieces. To shape each dragon, lightly dust your hands with confectioners' sugar and mold a piece of fondant into a ball. Roll between the palms of your hands to flatten and lengthen slightly. Pinch out a cherry-sized piece of fondant at one end, lengthening and flattening it slightly to shape a head. At the other end, pinch out and roll the fondant to a point for the tail. Pinch along the length of the fondant slightly for the back of the dragon. Using a small sharp knife, cut a horizontal slit for the mouth and press in the handle of a paintbrush to shape nostrils.

Secure the dragon to a cupcake with a dampened paintbrush, curving the head and tail around the edge slightly. Repeat to give 5 dragons. From the green fondant trimmings, shape pea-sized balls of fondant into small, flat triangles for pointed tails and flat feet. Use a small sharp knife to make indentations for toes.

Wings: Soften an Oreo™ cookie briefly in the microwave (see page 18). Scrape away the center and cut the biscuits in half with a small sharp knife. Using a $^3/_4$-inch (2-cm) round cookie cutter, cut out 3 semicircles from the straight edges to shape a pair of wings. Repeat with the remaining Oreo™ cookies to make 5 pairs. Cut a slit in each side of the dragons, pipe a little green decorator frosting into the openings, and press a wing into each.

Finishing touches: Using a small sharp knife, cut triangles of red chewy fruit roll. Pipe a line of red decorator frosting down the length of each dragon. Secure the triangles along the frosting, making them smaller as you work toward the tails. Cut out tongues from the trimmings and secure in place. Pipe small red claws onto the ends of the feet in red decorator frosting. Roll tiny balls of white fondant and secure in place for eyes. Use a paintbrush and green food coloring, or an icing pen, to paint the centers of the eyes.

Witch

Ingredients

- Black food coloring
- 1 quantity vanilla buttercream (see page 8)
- 5 cupcakes in black baking cups (see pages 6–7)
- 1³/₄ oz (50 g) lilac decorating sugar (see page 22)
- 1 large shredded whole wheat cereal biscuit
- 10 mini chocolate drops
- 5 red or pink gummy candies
- Tubes of black and red decorator frosting
- 5 Oreos™
- 6 tablespoons chocolate hazelnut spread
- 5 small square candies

Equipment

- Small sharp knife
- Small spatula
- Paper pastry bag (see page 25)
- Scissors

Preparing the cupcakes: Beat black food coloring into the vanilla buttercream, adding a little at a time until a pale gray shade is reached. Using a small spatula, spread a thin layer of buttercream over each cupcake as smoothly as possible. Place an additional 2 teaspoons of buttercream onto each cupcake and spread over the center, forming an oval shape. Taper to a point at one end for the witch's chin. Sprinkle lilac decorating sugar over the flat edges of the cupcakes, leaving the face areas clear.

Faces: Break up the shredded whole wheat cereal biscuit into pieces and push into the buttercream on each cupcake for hair. Add chocolate drops for eyes and cut off pieces of gummy candy for noses. Use the black decorator frosting to pipe eyebrows and red decorator frosting for lips. Pipe further dots of black decorator frosting over the cheeks and chin.

Hats: Gently split the mini Oreos™ in half, scrape off the white filling, and press one half on top of the hair. Secure in place with a little black decorator frosting. Put the chocolate hazelnut spread in a paper pastry bag and snip off the end about ¹/₄-inch (5 mm) from the tip. Pipe swirls of spread onto each hat. Position a square candy at the front and pipe a square on it in red decorator frosting.

Other ideas: Shape broomsticks by securing lengths of broken up shredded whole wheat cereal biscuit to the ends of 2-inch (5-cm) lengths of chocolate mint stick with decorator icing. Pipe bands of decorator frosting around the cereal to resemble string. Arrange over cupcakes decorated with dark-colored buttercream, and scattered with edible star- and moon-shaped sprinkles and gummy candies such as snakes and frogs.

WWWWWWHHHAAHAAHAAAAA!!

Spellbindingly
delicious

Scary cereal hair

Witchy fun

Jack O'Lantern

Ingredients

- 5 cupcakes in purple or black baking cups (see pages 6–7)
- 5 mini cupcakes (see page 7)
- 1 quantity vanilla buttercream (see page 8)
- 9 oz (250 g) orange rolled fondant
- Confectioners' sugar, for dusting
- 3 tablespoons lemon curd
- Tube of black decorator frosting
- Small piece of green rolled fondant

Equipment

- Small sharp knife
- Small spatula
- Rolling pin
- 4-inch (10-cm) round cookie cutter
- Fine paintbrush
- Paper pastry bag (see page 25)
- Scissors

Preparing the cupcakes: Cut the dome tops off each of the cupcakes. Using a small spatula, spread a thin layer of vanilla buttercream over the larger cupcakes. Invert a mini cupcake onto the top of each cupcake, remove the baking cup, and round off the edges to create a dome shape. Cover with a generous layer of buttercream.

Shaping the pumpkins: Roll out the orange rolled fondant on a surface lightly dusted with confectioners' sugar until about $1/16$ inch (2 mm) thick and then cut out 5 disks using a 4-inch (10-cm) round cookie cutter. (You'll need to reroll the trimmings to make enough disks). Position a disk over each cupcake, gently easing the fondant to fit around the sides. Trim off any excess fondant around the edges of the cups. Use the handle of a paintbrush to mark deep grooves over the fondant, as in the picture.

Pumpkin faces: Using a small sharp knife, cut out 2 eyes, a nose, and a mouth from each cupcake, and lift away the orange fondant from the centers. Put the lemon curd in a paper pastry bag and snip off the merest tip. Fill the eyes, nose, and mouth areas with the lemon curd. Use black decorator frosting to outline the edges.

Stalks: Shape the green fondant into 5 stalks and secure to the tops of the pumpkins using a dampened paintbrush. To finish, use a small sharp knife to mark a curved line around the stalks.

BOO!

Big smile!

where can I go for more scary fun?

Graveyard

Ingredients

- 1 quantity cream cheese frosting (see page 8)
- Green and black food coloring
- 5 cupcakes in black baking cups (see pages 6–7)
- 5 Oreo™ cookies
- 5 pink fruit chews
- 1 oz (25 g) semisweet chocolate, grated
- Tubes of red, yellow, and white decorator frosting

Equipment

- Small spatula
- Scissors
- Paper pastry bag (see page 25)
- Small sharp knife
- Toothpicks
- Fine paintbrush

Grass: Reserve 2 tablespoons of the cream cheese frosting. Beat green food coloring into the remaining frosting, adding a little at a time until the desired shade is reached. Using a small spatula, spread the frosting over each cupcake, building it up a little on one half to form a mound. Press a hole into the center of each mound with your fingertip.

Gravestones: Carefully soften the Oreo™ cookies in the microwave (see page 23). Scrap aways the white filling then, using scissors, cut two straight sides off each cookie. Beat black food coloring into the reserved frosting, adding a little at a time until pale gray. Put in a paper pastry bag and snip off the merest tip. Pipe a thin line of frosting around the edge of each cookie, then a second line and a small cross in the center of the "gravestone."

Limbs: Soften the pink fruit chews in the microwave for a few seconds if too firm to mold (see page 20). Mold each into a sausage shape about $1^3/4$ inches (4 cm) long. Flatten one end to shape a hand. Pinch in at the wrists. Cut out finger shapes using a small sharp knife. Push a toothpick up through the limb for support, then press the other end of the toothpick into the hole in the "grass" mound. Repeat with the 4 remaining cupcakes.

Finishing touches: On each cupcake, press a gravestone into the frosting behind the limb. (If necessary, prop up the gravestone with a toothpick until it sets in position.) Sprinkle the grated semisweet chocolate over the grass mounds, pressing it down gently. Sprinkle more grated chocolate over the hand areas. Use a paintbrush and green food coloring to paint green marks over the limbs. Pipe simple flower shapes on the grass in red, yellow, and white decorator frosting.

Cookie tombstone

Reach for the sky

Rest in chocolate

Ghost

Ingredients

- 4¹/₂ oz (125 g) fondant sugar
- Black food coloring
- 5 cupcakes in blue baking cups (see pages 6–7)
- 3¹/₂ oz (100 g) white fruit chews
- Black decorating sugar (see page 22)

Equipment

- Small spatula
- Toothpicks
- Fine paintbrush

Preparing the cakes: Put the fondant sugar in a bowl and beat in a little water at a time until the liquid fondant thickly coats the back of the spoon. Beat in black food coloring, adding a little at a time until a pale gray shade is reached. Using a small spatula, spread the fondant over the tops of the cupcakes, letting it run down the sides slightly.

Ghosts: For each ghost, soften ³/₄ oz (20 g) fruit chews in the microwave for a few seconds if too firm to mold (see page 20). Mold the fruit chews into an oval shape, then flatten out slightly, adding a little peak at one end and trailing it down to a point at the other. Using your fingers, make soft indentations to create a ghostly form (see opposite). Bend in half and sit one ghost on each cupcake so the pointed end comes over the side. Prop up the shapes until firm with toothpicks inserted into the cupcakes.

Finishing touches: Using a paintbrush and black food coloring, paint a pair of large eyes and a smiling mouth on each ghost. Sprinkle black decorating sugar over the gray fondant on each cupcake.

Try me too! page 42

OOOOOOOOOOOOOOOoooooo

Cheerful ghost

Frighteningly fantastic

Skull and Bones

Ingredients

- 3$^{1}/_{2}$ oz (100 g) white chocolate, chopped
- 5 cupcakes in purple baking cups (see pages 6–7)
- Black food coloring
- 1 quantity vanilla buttercream (see page 8)

Equipment

- Parchment paper
- Paper pastry bag (see page 25)
- Scissors
- Toothpick
- Small spatula

Skull and bones: Trace the skull and bones template (see page 127) onto parchment paper. Lay a second, larger sheet of parchment paper over the traced outlines. Melt the chocolate (see page 00), then put in a paper pastry bag and snip off the merest tip. Pipe a thin line of chocolate around the edges of the shapes. Slide the top sheet of parchment over a little and pipe more shapes. (You'll need 6 or 7 skulls and about 55 bones, allowing for some spares in case of breakages.) Once all the outlines are done, fill in the centers, spreading the chocolate into the corners with a toothpick. Leave the shapes to harden in a cool place or refrigerate for at least 1 hour.

Preparing the cupcakes: Beat black food coloring into the vanilla buttercream, adding a little at a time until the desired shade is reached. Using a small spatula, spread buttercream over each cupcake as smoothly as possible, doming it slightly in the center.

Finishing touches: Carefully peel the parchment paper away from the bone and skull shapes. Gently press the bones around the edges of the cupcakes and a skull in each center.

Scary skull

A very dark place

Chocolate bones

Templates

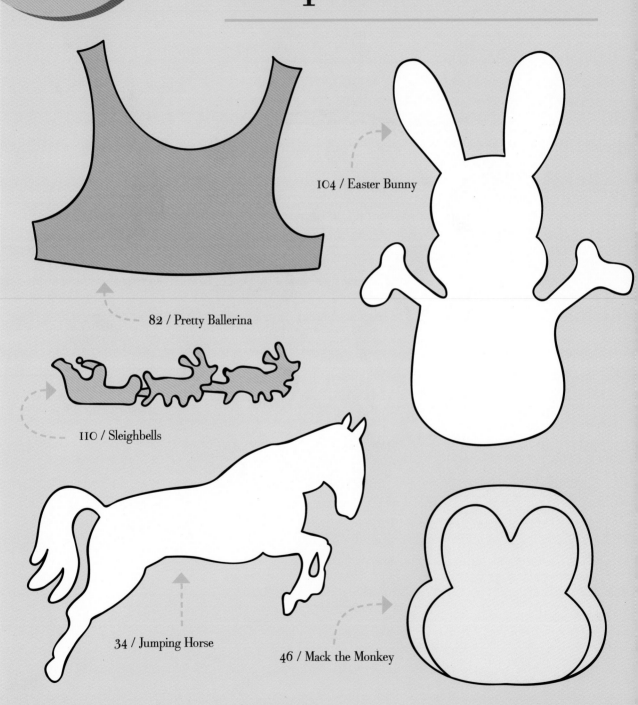

104 / Easter Bunny

82 / Pretty Ballerina

110 / Sleighbells

34 / Jumping Horse

46 / Mack the Monkey